If I'm *Crazy*,
I Am In Good Company

Using Our Intuitive Awareness

By I. R. Plummer

If I'm Crazy, I Am In Good Company

Published by

I. R. Plummer

The stories in this book are true. To protect the privacy of individuals names preceded with an * have been changed. All other names are given with the permission of those individuals and their websites and Facebook pages are listed in the directory at the back of the book.

Author website:
irplummer.com

Cover Designs by:
Rhonda (I.R.) Plummer

Background Designs by:
Stockxchng - www.sxc.hu
Blue background - ilco – 1112025
Red background - MidnightA - 1354424

If I'm Crazy, I Am In Good Company

Table of Contents

If I'm Crazy, I Am In Good Company

Acknowledgments

The foundation for this book started with an awareness of a creator that does not judge or limit the souls awareness. God and enlightened souls, or guides and angels if preferred, have held my hand, waited patiently, and trusted that the information and insights presented to me would be used to help others on their journey. For that trust and the faith that I would do this book justice I am eternally grateful.

When starting this book, I had no idea whom I would meet along the path, or how deeply they would touch my soul. The gifted individual's who shared their stories, and had faith in me as an intuitive and as a writer, is humbling. To each of you, I say thank you.

Marcey Hamm is an extraordinary artist whose inspiring music has kept me spiritually grounded during the process of writing and editing. Thank you.

A special thank you to Sonja Torres, owner of the Alternative For Healing website, for her help and insight.

If I'm Crazy, I Am In Good Company

Chapter 1

Introduction

The checklist part of life, the one that can be listed on social media without embarrassment, is straightforward; military brat, wife, mother, laughter, good memories and a few heartaches. Between piano lessons and school carpools, I was an insurance agent, entrepreneur, artist, and sales representative. During spare seconds, a basketful of college credits in business, counseling and psychology added interest and diversity to the pot. Over time, beliefs and personal truths merged, and led me to become a certified hypnotherapist, life counselor, Reiki master, mediator and author.

The part of me that was never discussed until I was past voting age…is more complex.

At a very young age, when my mother talked to ladies in the neighborhood, I heard answers to questions posed. The questions would have been well beyond the knowledge of a three or four year old, but that did not stop me from blurting out what I heard. When not hushed or scolded for interrupting, I eagerly shared how a voice whispered in my ear, and pretty pictures floated and shimmered before me. At that age, comments about an overactive imagination, sounded like a bad thing. Combined with lectures about lying, I stopped sharing what I saw and heard.

At thirteen, my father was transferred to California and once again I was the 'new kid'. One day, two girls I barely knew were discussing boys I did not know. A vision and my inner voice gave me information about what triggered a fistfight that landed two boys in the base hospital. I do not know why I decided to break my silence, but I started the comment with a 'maybe' to make it sound like I was throwing out an idea with no foundation. How I phrased the information did not matter; when my comment turned out to be factual the girls never spoke to me again.

Again, I vowed to keep my knowledge to myself, but silence fought a battle with the conviction that girlfriends struggling through situations and asking questions wanted truthful answers. What if, have you thought, it is possible and maybe, became the commonly used lead-in to present information in a package friends accepted without questions.

Over time, my intuitive abilities became an open secret; those who were open-minded knew or at least had an idea. Friends and family who thought psychic and witchcraft were synonyms or who rejected the idea of communication with a higher being were never told.

There was a time when I would have denied the idea of life experiences leading me towards a life I had never imagined; I would have been wrong. What I have learned is that life is a continual offering of choices and opportunities that without conscious thought build a foundation of beliefs and experiences. With hindsight, the twisted path that leads us where we need to go makes perfect sense.

After stepping away from organized religions, I purchased a book about Edgar Casey's life. I still own that book, and the library quickly expanded to include authors with a wide range of intuitive experiences. After becoming a hypnotherapist, I held workshops and taught adult education classes. I was the teacher, but in teaching I was also the student expanding my knowledge and intuitive abilities.

Then, in what seemed to happen without any inkling that life was about to change, I was pushed to take the next step.

In the first week of August 2013, a dream, so vivid that it resonated as fact, pushed me awake at dawn. Not being a chirpy morning person, I started coffee, propped myself against the counter and zoned out while it brewed.

When the coffee machine gurgled out the last drop of caffeine I filled a large mug and walked a few feet to a room filled with books and comfortable chairs. Sitting in an old oak rocker, I watched the sun cast its first light over the lawn and a labyrinth where a determined dandelion poked through the pea gravel. The sun creeping across the grass was soothing, but the sun and the infusion of caffeine did not have my full attention. Hovering over the labyrinth was a giant white screen, like you would see at an old drive-in movie theater. The feature film was a replay of the dream that pushed me awake.

In the dream, I am surrounded by a light with very pale overtones of blue, pink and yellow. The colors shimmer with a silver overlay, much like mother-of-pearl. The colors also flowed as if they breathed of life's harmony.

Silence embraces me with warmth and energy that vibrates from within me or around me, I'm not sure which.

Before me, large masculine hands with long fingers and trim nails appeared. I will not deny or claim that the illuminated hands were God's, but I knew I was standing before a presence who offered unconditional love and the hands held power and tenderness. Clouds with a slight blue cast formed sleeves. The deep drape and folds reminded me of a Wizard's robe. The hands were palms up. At the elbows the arms fade and blend with the background. Cradled in the hands, like a precious baby, is a book. If I'm Crazy, I Am In Good Company, is printed in bold print at the top of the book. I have a sense that the book is already written and showing it to me is significant. When I see the author's name splashed across the bottom, denial, panic or both push me fully awake.

For several years, I have written and published mystery novels with a paranormal twist. Fiction has a beginning, middle, and an ending. Adding what society labels 'psychic' powers, without the need to admit that some of the experiences are personal is safe, and fun.

Instinctively, I knew what the book was about and balked at the idea. Exposing my truths to strangers with a deep wealth of criticism and skepticism makes me contemplate the definition of insanity.

As a teen, when a minster stated that psychics and people who studied astrology were card carrying members of the devil's workshop, I expected lightning to strike me dead in the pew. Certain that when the minister's eyes met mine he saw me as Satin's assistant; I avoided talking to him when possible. Years later, similar comments, repeated by ministers, preachers and priests, forced me to reevaluate organized religions.

Scientists and physicians have written thousands of articles that depict psychics as mentally unbalanced and dangerous. I have been around mentally unbalanced, and can say with confidence that I do not qualify. As for dangerous, the only thing I have ever harmed is a computer keyboard.

I have met many people who act like their intuitive abilities are dusted with fairy dust, and they usually had a posse of followers to stroke their ego and help feed the half-truths and lies. I have also watched people use verbal abuse to destroy the reputations of people who dare to contradict their beliefs. Alone those are enough reasons to keep silent, as a whole the backlash is enough to cause nightmares. So my reluctance has merit.

For two weeks, I tried to ignore the original dream and subsequent dreams that showed me promoting the book. Still, the artistic side of my nature wanted to flow freely and openly trust that the dream was showing me what was meant to be, a finished book. Like the determined dandelion in the labyrinth my thoughts grew, blossomed, and produced seeds that grew into what if possibilities and questions. The questions produced interest, more questions, and finally one serious thought.

How do you write a book when there is no real beginning, and no ending?

"One word at a time." The purr of the voice whispering in my ear held a dose of humor.

"Cute!" I muttered and headed for the coffee pot.

Chapter 2

Intuitive Awareness

Intuition is a gut feeling or knowingness, based on little or no concrete information that helps a person reach a conclusion. Intuitive awareness goes a step further by accepting the conclusion as factual and proceeding to act on the information.

It is human nature to put objects and food into tidy airtight containers or boxes and label them. That works well for salt, sugar and rat poison. It also helps when looking for a particular pair of shoes, a box filled with old comic books, or a shoe box full of marbles. However, when Star Wars figurines, Hot Wheels, Barbie dolls and Beanie Babies are put into one box and the box is labeled 'toys,' there is no way to know the actual contents of the box without looking inside.

Like the box of miscellaneous toys, some labels have grown to include a multitude of items and abilities. Psychic is such a word.

The Merriam Webster Dictionary's (free internet edition) description of psychic is; adjective; used to describe strange mental powers and abilities (such as the ability to predict the future, to know what other people are thinking, or to receive messages from dead people) that cannot be explained by natural laws.

The ability to predict the future, to read minds and talk to the dead; that means the word psychic is a label for miscellaneous intuitive abilities. Like the box marked toys, the miscellaneous label is confusing and tells a person little about a particular intuitive ability.

The New World Encyclopedia (internet edition) states that the role and definition of natural law has varied widely throughout history. The definition of natural law is: the law of nature (Latin) is law whose content derives naturally from human nature or physical nature, and therefore has universal validity...In ethical theory, certain choices, actions or dispositions might be asserted to be inhuman, unnaturally cruel, perverse, or unreasonable from a moral point of view.

If natural law is derived naturally from human or physical nature, who determines what is natural? The answer does not include individuals who use their psychic powers because if that were true, intuitive abilities would be readily accepted instead of described as 'strange mental powers'.

Society accepts that we are born with five senses; audio (hearing), sight, taste, touch and smell. Without thought to the enormous infrastructure that makes communication between the senses possible, we take these senses, and the ability for them to connect and work simultaneously for granted.

Why shouldn't normal include acceptance that we are born with the same abilities on a higher realm of consciousness? The easy answer is that unlike the accepted five senses, the higher senses are brief moments of awareness. Having a brief vision of a monkey driving a car, or a nurse smelling roses in a sterile operating room, cannot be verified. A complex and self-serving answer, is greed and power. If people used their intuitive abilities to 'read' people's true intentions, the ability to control through propaganda and fear would be minimal.

Shortly after the dream about this book, I asked people browsing through an estate sale if they would tell me their understanding of psychic. The method of research involved a yellow sheet of paper and hash marks next to repetitive answers, effective, but not scientific.

Fourteen people said someone who talks to ghosts. Twenty-three people thought a psychic could read a person's mind. With no obvious fear or distain for the concept of paranormal abilities, these individuals answered the question before asking the reason behind the question. After telling them I was doing research for a book, several people shared personal experiences or those of family and friends.

Nineteen individuals said Devil's work, Satanism, the Occult, voodoo, the evil eye, witchcraft, trickery, and anti-Christian or anti-biblical beliefs. With preconceived ideas of paranormal abilities being based in evil or anti-spiritualism, everyone in this group wanted an explanation before answering the question. From this group, I received stories about people taking advantage of the emotionally weak. Psychics were called mentally unbalanced, and liars looking for attention. One man talked about a relative with bipolar disorder; she had conversations with a deceased relative. Several people said they would pray for me, and I was offered a church business card, a Watchtower magazine, and a Book of Mormon. One woman looked pointedly at her twelve year old daughter and made a comment about over active imaginations.

The definitions, like the label, tell a story of beliefs that have been shaped by family, experiences, religion, movies, governments, educators, and ignorance. The underlying factor to these beliefs is fear of the unknown, and the ability of authoritative figures to utilize fear to control people's beliefs, money, and actions.

From birth, we are students who take what is offered and mix it with personal experiences. That combination makes a foundation for personal beliefs and emotional balance. When appropriate, we become the teacher, but everyone's experiences are slightly different. My truths, the life stories shared by other talented intuitive individuals, and the information shared in this book offer an opportunity for a person to mold their beliefs into what is right for them.

Life in its present state on earth is an evolution—birth, growth, death. The growth of bones is limited, but the growth of the mind is limitless because life experiences and the ability to build new memories is a daily process. Some of the information presented may sound similar to personal stories. If so, instead of limiting the experience, expand the horizon to explore the internal you.

The subconscious is a direct link to a person's soul memory, the filing cabinet of information that knows the bare bones, oh-my-gosh you. Each night, in dreams, the soul takes an extraordinary journey to connect with the real you, and your extraordinary intuitive powers. These breaks from reality help neutralize negative energy and keep the spirit balanced and healthy.

However, tapping into the subconscious is not a mystery that only works in the witching hour of the night. People who accept and use the higher realm of intuitive senses can connect with the soul level of conscious when needed. Learning how begins with an open-mind to possibilities and a willingness to explore what lies beyond the narrow realm of conscious reality.

Everyone has intuitive powers—no exceptions! Using these abilities takes acceptance and practice. An artist's first attempts at painting a portrait may resemble a stick figure or a paint-by-number painting that is stiff and lifeless. Only with practice and patience, will perception and the ability to fill in the finer details become a natural process. For most people, intuitive powers work the same way. Recognition of a whisper in the ear, the gut feeling or a flash of insight, will lead to more intuitive insights. With time, the abilities shift, until an intuitive ability becomes stronger or all the senses work equally well.

No matter how, or at what age intuitive powers first appear, each person perceives and receives information differently. That makes a person's intuitive talent unique to them. When working with information shared in books, on the internet, workshops, and in seminars, a person should adjust the techniques to work comfortably with their intuitive abilities.

The word psychic is misleading. The idea of having, 'strange mental powers' reminds me of, *My Favorite Martian*, a television comedy in the 1960's, or people wearing tinfoil hats, comical but incorrect.

I prefer to call psychic powers; intuitive abilities or intuitive powers. Like the ability to breathe without the need to think about inhaling and exhaling, we can use the intuitive ability or consciously choose to ignore them.

Using intuitive awareness is an unconscious acceptance that there is an emotional, physical and unknown depth to the mind and body that cannot be scientifically proven. At the subconscious level, emotional growth and spiritual awareness can have a more profound effect. That inner awareness can affect the conscious level of awareness, and change beliefs and actions.

Imagine Christmas and birthday presents that come in many sizes and shapes. Some gifts are wrapped in brightly colored paper that will grab a person's attention and imagination. Some presents are wrapped in humble brown paper bags that are deceptive in the simplicity.

As a gift, intuitive powers are no different. Simple or star studded impressive, we can choose to use the gifts, share the gifts, or leave them in the box to collect dust.

A large box with a bright red bow is flashy and captures people's attention and imagination. Intuitive gifts that attract attention are mediums helping the police track down a killer or locate a missing child. For days, the news will play every angle of the story and will mention the stories with each new story of a lost child located with the help of a person's gut feeling or intuitive abilities. Adding to the media circus, tabloid magazines, set next to every cash register in the universe, will twist the stories into shocking headlines about two-headed psychics with a third eye in the middle of their foreheads.

Television shows about time travel, mediums, witches, shape shifters, werewolves and vampires captivate audiences around the world. The sensationalized attraction of these shows brings aspects of intuitive powers into public awareness. Romance novels portray shape shifters, vampires and werewolves as muscle bound men looking for the right female to tame their lustful and blood thirsty instincts. Science fiction novels have these same creatures living next door and keeping our world safe from the evil amongst us. These ideas are entertaining but they also generate ideas that have little or nothing to do with reality.

Understated gifts, delivered without fanfare, are easy to overlook or dismiss as nonsense. Early one morning, on a twisty mountain pass in Nevada, my 'voice within' warned me to slow down. The road was icy and the curves were tight, so slowing down meant barely moving. Around the next curve, a jackknifed semi-trailer blocked both lanes of the road. The wheels on the bright purple cab were still spinning. The driver was struggling to get out of the drivers doors window. Slowing down added no more than thirty seconds to the time it took to maneuver the curve, but those precious seconds prevented a more serious accident.

It is not uncommon to hear stories about a car pulling out of a side road or running a stop sign seconds after a gut feeling made a person slowdown or stop. Yet, if people gave credit to their inner voice or stated that their higher intuitive powers saved them from injury, few people would accept the story as factual. Instead, the story would be considered nonsense or a lie.

Friends who owned a janitorial business in Los Angeles left a job at four in the morning. Besides the couple, two employees were in the van. Normally, *Lance made a right turn out of the parking garage and a second right at a nearby intersection. One night, Lance had a gut feeling, nothing specific just an unease. Believing the feeling was a warning, he turned left instead of right out of the parking garage. Seconds later, the pop-pop-pop of gunfire filled the still night air. One of the employees stuck his head out a window to look behind them. At the intersection, men with rifles were running across the street. The morning news was filled with details about a gang war, and death.

Whether it is a near miss traffic accident or a close brush with death, the intuitive incidents will not make the nightly news, but that does not make the gift of intuition and audio perception any less significant.

When asked what they want to be when they grow up, it is not unusual for children to mention age appropriate fantasies like being a Red Ninja Turtle or Cinderella. With maturity, the dreams of being a rock star when the person is tone deaf, or an astronaut when they are terrified of heights, fade. But sometimes a dream outshines the reality of what would really make a person happy. Whether intuition steps in and heads a person down the right path or fate plays the starring role, is a matter of perspective and attitude.

While attending college to earn a counseling degree, I worked at a counseling center filing insurance claims. Files for patients, who after years of therapy, still had not found closure to emotional issues, and talks with the counselors, taught me that my idea of emotional healing and the medical professions idea of emotional healing were light years apart.

Unwilling to compromise my beliefs, I researched alternatives. Alchemical hypnotherapy, an interactive process of helping a person connect with their soul memory, interested me. The idea of using interactive hypnosis to quickly identify the core root of a problem, instead of spending years talking about or around an issue, made sense. Research put the closest school, five hundred miles away. Too far to walk to on a sunny day, the idea was put on hold.

Two years later, the company where I worked, unexpectedly closed the branch office. That same day, I was offered a temporary position. I came very close to turning the job down, but my 'voice within' kept saying, 'it's only four months, do it.' That evening my parents' mentioned that they needed a house sitter for a month. After a day full of unforeseen events, it was no surprise that the temporary job ended a week before my parents' vacation.

I arrived at my parents' home in California on a Wednesday. On Thursday, I called the owner of an alchemical hypnotherapy school hoping he could tell me about a class closer to home. In my dream list of wants, I had not clarified whose home. He mentioned a new school in Sacramento that was starting a class the following day—they had one opening.

Think about this, every step that took me to school was unplanned, yet each step fit into the next step like a precision cut puzzle piece.

I call this intuitive persistence; the guiding forces that take us where we need to be even when a dream would lead down a different path.

I have heard many stories about how unseen forces guided a person to a new job or a new relationship. For most that meant watching a dream die; which is never easy. With time to emotionally heal and the clarity of hindsight, these same individuals were able to identify the lessons learned and appreciate the journey.

*Kelly's story is a good example and one many people can identify with.

Kelly, a thirty something masseuse at a day spa in Phoenix, told me she was raised in a small town and grew up dreaming of a life in New York City working in advertising. Shortly after graduating from high school, she was offered the opportunity to attend massage therapy school for free, she declined.

The following week, the owner of the bakery where she worked, announced his retirement and closure of the shop. Shortly after that, her car broke down—the repairs took a big chunk of her savings. With no job prospects, her parents' asked her to move to Phoenix to spend the summer with her grandmother who had recently had a stroke.

Disheartened, she moved in with her grandmother, and accepted the offer to attend the massage therapy school.

During the first week of classes, she started having visions of muscles tied in knots and a hammer beating on a head or lower back. Thinking she would use what she thought of as a 'dead-end job pampering the rich' to fund her move to New York, she thought the vivid daydreams were her way of dealing with frustration and disappointment.

Since the stroke, Kelly's grandmother had suffered from a headache that throbbed at her temples. One evening, while Kelly gave her a massage, the grandmother asked how she knew the headache had shifted and now hammered against the back of her neck. Kelly realized she had used a vision of the neck and the soft 'voice within,' that she thought was a mental replay of the teacher's instructions, to guide her.

She was unconvinced that what happened was more than a fluke, but she started to pay attention to the visions and the inner voice. She said if she listened, the information given was accurate. When she allowed doubt to invade her thoughts she made mistakes.

As for moving to New York City, she laughed. She and two friends owned the day spa and were preparing to open a second location. She said it was the best advice her 'inner voice' had given.

When asked if she would have been just as happy working in advertising, her response was a quick 'no.' Kelly created the advertising for the spas, but a few freelance jobs showed that her artistic creativity and ability to create catchy jingles was limited to things she felt strongly about.

Intuitive persistence worked in a slightly different way for a highway patrolman I met at a surprise birthday party. This was before cellphones, so there was no way to know exactly when the guest of honor would arrive. Yet, when I suggested that we turn off the lights a full ten minutes before *Bob was expected, no one argued. Nor did anyone act surprised when Bob's unmarked patrol car pulled into the driveway a couple of minutes later.

When the commotion settled down, *Greg, a highway patrolman, drew me aside and asked how long I had known I was psychic. Not being a question I was often asked, I hesitated, but logic said only another person who used their intuitive abilities would ask. Greg nodded and gave a knowing smile when I admitted that visions and what I call, instant messages, had always been a part of my life.

Greg grew up knowing he wanted to be a lawyer. He went to law school and set up practice with his father. By the end of the first year, he was miserable. The problem was his intuitive gifts were finely tuned, and he used them to judge a person's character. Not the best intuitive power when people want a lawyer to twist laws in their favor.

Greg saw auras, and within the aura he saw a shift in color when someone lied. After a long talk with his father, he left the law firm. With an easy laugh, he told me using his abilities to put the guilty behind bars was more fun and allowed him to sleep easily.

His lie detector skills had a low margin of error. One hindrance was caused by a person's indecisiveness. In that second of indecision when he asked me about being psychic, he saw the aura between my heart and hip shift to a darker hue. When I decided to be truthful, the shadow cleared. He also found that proficient liars, those that believed their lies, were able to control their emotions. With no remorse, their aura did not change color when they lied.

Another intuitive power Greg used regularly is hard to define. When on patrol, he allowed an inner knowledge to direct where he drove. He told me it was not a voice or even a gut feeling, it was simply a knowing that he needed to drive south or turn off at an exit and head north. In doing that, more often than not, he was in the position to be where he was needed.

Enhancing Intuitive Powers

To develop or fine-tune intuitive powers, three inner tools work together to create the path to awareness.

The first tool is trust. Acceptance that what is seen, sensed, or heard is coming from a higher source, not personal thoughts or the mental feedback of people who would like nothing better than to see us fail.

The second tool is listening, and knowing the difference between inner demons, personal thoughts and the 'voice within.' Most of the time, my 'voice within' is masculine, so there is no second guessing about who is 'talking.' If you cannot tell the difference between the 'voice within' and your mother scolding you for sneaking a cookie before dinner, listen to what is said. Also think about the tone of the delivery; is it harsh and critical or calm and supportive? Then decide if the comments are valid, and whether or not you should act upon the information.

The third tool is practice. Practice provides confidence that what is seen, sensed, or felt, is real. Do not expect practice to create perfection because it is human nature to question, hesitate, procrastinate, ignore, jump to conclusions, and at times want instant gratification without caring about the consequences that are sure to follow rash decisions.

Thanks to technology, cruise control will keep a cars speedometer within an acceptable range of the posted speed limit. That was not always the case, so my 'voice within' likes to announce the location of patrol cars. It is not uncommon for me to hear, 'a cop is five miles ahead, speed trap ahead,' or 'the car behind or ahead of you is unmarked.' When that happens, I check the accuracy of the information. Usually, a police cruiser is within range of the information given, but not always.

After receiving incorrect information, it would be easy to ignore the information the next time it is given, but acting on a warning to drive a different road to work or slow down, cannot hurt. Whereas not listening or reacting just to test whether or not the information was incorrect is not worth the gamble of living with 'if only' regrets.

Ignoring skepticism is not a tool, but it takes practice. To overcome the tendency to ignore the 'voice within' I turned each comment into a true or false question and recorded the information in a spiral binder. Not all the information given has an immediate answer, so the information was checked weekly. Over a twelve month period, I found that the accuracy of the information was over ninety percent correct. The remaining information held bits of truth mixed with events that did not come to pass.

When receiving information about a friend, the desire is to give them positive information, encouragement to work towards a goal or positive feedback on emotional issues or work. However, censoring information received may give a person false hope that prolongs a bad situation.

When a woman asked me if purchasing a nail salon was a good idea, she was pleased to hear that the business was solid. Because she was very close to a sister-in-law, it was tempting not to add that a business partnership with her was a bad idea. The warning did not set well, but the woman talked to her lawyer. A year later, when the sister-in-law tried to include her share of the business in a divorce settlement, the revisions that had been made to the business contract paid off.

In addition to relating the exact words or details, not jumping to conclusions is important. A vision of a man having lunch with a female other than his wife does not necessarily mean they are having an affair. Nor does seeing a bald man or woman mean they are undergoing chemotherapy.

I also try to avoid answering questions that ask for an opinion. Yes, I have an opinion, but how I interpret a situation and how the receiver interprets the scene will most likely be different. For example, when telling a single woman I saw a pregnant woman playing with two young boys, I thought I was being shown a future event in her life. The truth was, a sister she closely resembled, had two young sons and was hoping to have a third child. A week after that 'reading' the sister-in-law confirmed that she was pregnant.

When not talking to someone at the time of a vision, and if what is being shown does not relate to my thoughts, I write the details in a notebook. The vision may be related to a client due that day or a phone call, but just as likely the answer will not appear for days, weeks or months.

There is a difference between a daydream where anything is possible, and hopes and desires that are grounded in a spark of reality. A daydream of getting a job as an astronaut is possible. If the daydream is more centered on meeting Mr. Spock and being the captain of the Enterprise, it is a fantasy break from reality.

The same is true for interpreting a vision. If hope and desires distort how information is interpreted it is like trying to force a false answer into a truth, it does not work!

For example; a person is told that a vision shows him sitting on a sunny beach being served a cocktail by a butler dressed in a powder blue tux. The person, who dreams of retiring before they turn forty, interprets this to mean they are going to win the lottery, but they also are grounded in reality. Instead of stopping at the bank to cash out their savings to purchase lottery tickets, they gamble two dollars. When they arrive home, there is a message on the answer-machine saying they won a contest. The prize is a vacation in the Caribbean.

The chance of that vision being interpreted correctly was slim, which is why I used it; not all visions are supposed to be understood. Sometimes visions are a warning to let daydreams be fun escapes and pay more attention to the everyday details that can build dreams.

The same is true when a person has unrealistic expectations; the chance of the reality and the expectation matching are slim. Information received through intuitive powers may confirm expectations or show a dream becoming reality. Yet, if a person allows expectations to blur reality, disappointment is the result.

For example, hypnotherapy clients make appointments to lose weight, and expect one session to change years of poor eating habits. People also want to believe that changing one area of their life will not affect every aspect of their life. When reality sets in, they blame others for their failure, instead of admitting they had expectations of instant cures without having to do any work or address the issues that caused stress and distress.

No matter how many different ways a question is asked, visions and intuitive information cannot be manipulated to create a desired reality. If the vision does change, the person has side-stepped intuitive and stepped into a daydream or mental feedback.

Everyone is born with higher realm intuitive abilities. The choice to ignore, deny or use the powers is a process that starts at an early age. Without outside influence, the decision to accept and use intuitive abilities would be an easy one. Sadly, few people are born into an environment that does not influence decisions—including whether or not intuitive abilities are fact or fiction.

If a person is on a quest, and expects intuitive abilities to lead them down a garden path scattered with rose petals, lottery numbers, perfect relationships, perfect health, and instant answers to any number of annoying questions, they will be deeply disappointed.

Instead, think of intuitive abilities as gifts to be used in daily in practical ways and to be shared with others. In return, you will be offered golden gems of wisdom to guide you, and you will discover life changing opportunities.

I believe that if intuitive abilities were not met with skepticism, ridicule and fear, more people would admit that they use their higher powers at work and personally. Even if the information received is not used daily, at the least, the information would be considered and like Lauraine F., judgment and actions would be based on the information given.

Lauraine, a wife, mother, and small business owner, lives in Missouri. Her experiences echo many people whose intuitive abilities are subtle aspects of their daily life. Without conscious thought, they accept and use their gifts, but do not openly discuss how they receive information and guidance.

In Lauraine's words, here is her story.

"When I was young, I thought everyone had the same capabilities, I could feel a person's distress or pain, and I often heard their thoughts. At a very young age, I would hear my mother's thoughts and respond. For instance, I would be in my bedroom or outside and would hear my mother ask a question. Locating her, I would answer the question. Years later, she admitted that each time it happened she was surprised. Although my comments were always related to her thoughts, she had not verbally spoken, and her thoughts were not necessarily directed at me.

"As a child, vivid dreams, seeing spirits, telepathic communication and smelling odd odors when the air was clear, were not discussed. So, I assumed they were common abilities that everyone had. I do not know at what age I realized that was not true, but as I matured the experiences did not happen as often.

"As a young bride, I joined my husband's church. The religion preached that paranormal experiences were demonic. Due to church's teachings, for almost twenty years I was afraid to mention my experiences.

"In 2000, after leaving the church, I started to pay attention to what I saw, sensed, smelled, and felt. Eventually, I realized that my intuitive abilities never shutdown, I had simply ignored the information and repressed the memories.

"I receive a lot of information in dreams. When I was three, my younger sister died. Shortly after she passed, she came to me in a dream. In the dream, she was an adult, and she said, 'it is all going to be okay.' At three, I did not know why she was giving me reassurance, but over the years I have found comfort in her words.

"In another dream, a male friend, whom I had been very close to, appeared. The dream was short, and at the end he said good-bye. The following day, I found out that he died around the time I had the dream. Knowing that he came to say good-bye has continued to be a comfort.

"Once as a child, and several times as a teenager, I saw a shadow in the bedroom window. The window was ten feet from the ground, and there was no tree by the window. Yet, I clearly saw the head and shoulder silhouette of a person. Occurring before I fell asleep, the sightings were not a dream or a daydream. Instead of the shadow freaking me out, I found the experiences comforting. Each time it happened, I fell into deep relaxing sleep. I still have no explanation for what happened, but the comfort was real and helped me through some difficult times.

"Since childhood, I have known a woman who lives just a few miles from my home. Her kitchen has a very distinct aroma, one I cannot describe but is probably a combination of spices and years of cooking. One day while standing in my kitchen, I could smell the aroma of her kitchen. I thought about calling her, but instead dismissed the incident.

"The next week, I saw her in town and mentioned the incident. She looked surprised and said she had been in a car accident that day. As we parted, she asked that if it happened again to contact her immediately because she would need me.

"Two years later, on a Saturday morning, the aroma filled my kitchen. I called her immediately. In emotional distress over a family situation, she needed to talk. We are not related and seldom see each other, so I do not know why the intuitive connection between us is strong, but I do not question why.

"One day, I drove down a road I have been on hundreds of times. I am empathic, meaning I can feel other people's emotions, but I was alone in the car, so there was no apparent reason for me to be overwhelmed with a gut-wrenching sadness. Scanning the sides of the road, I saw a cemetery that I did not remember seeing before. More likely, with no reason to remember the cemetery, years of familiarity meant I drove on automatic reflexes as I processed the day's events or what needed to be done next.

"Glancing at the cemetery a second time, the pain intensified. Deciding to investigate, I discovered a small cemetery with a loop driveway. The pain was sharp as I drove by one section, but I continued to drive around the loop. The pain decreased until I reached the spot a second time. Walking the grounds, I was physically alone, but it felt like I had startled someone. It is a bad pun, but like I had walked over someone's grave.

"Using the energy causing me discomfort as a guide, I headed towards the core of the energy and stopped where the energy felt the strongest. I stood by a headstone of a young man who died in his early twenties. Like static electricity, the energy around the grave brought goose-bumps to my arms and the hair on the back of my neck tingled.

"Without knowing what to do, I silently asked if the emotions I felt were coming from him. I felt his presence, but there was no communication. Not knowing what else to do, I walked back to my car. As I reached the car I heard, 'please tell them I'm lonely.' Like a chant, the words were repeated several times.

"At home, I did some research on the internet. The boy had died in an auto accident. I thought about contacting the family, but never made the call. A few days after my initial visit, I returned to the cemetery. Someone had left a sticky note on his headstone, and his presence was no longer there.

"Another way I use my empathic abilities is to sense a person's emotional state. Not the smile they display for the public, but the deeper emotions that are masked by the ready smile. When working with the public, I use that to temper my responses. I have also found that I can radiate positive energy to help people who are depressed or unhappy. That is really great because it is a ripple effect, whatever you send out pops back to you."

If I'm Crazy, I Am In Good Company

Chapter 3

Audio / Clairaudience

Jingle Bells, Jingle Bells, Jingle all....

I apologize to those that had to sing the song to the end, but it made a point. We all have a voice that speaks within. Some people say it is like a whisper in the ear. Others describe the voice as originating from the crown of the head, or the third eye. This telepathic communication is a natural and easy way for guides and angels to offer advice, answer questions, and try to steer us away from trouble. The voice is within us, but it is not our personal thoughts, so I refer to it as the 'voice within'.

As a small child, I thought the voice whispering in my ear was Tinker Bell. It made sense that if she could fly and talk to Peter Pan, she could be invisible, and sit on my shoulder to share her knowledge. The 'voice within' still feels like someone whispering in my ear, but now the voice is masculine.

At a picnic, a four-year-old boy shared a story about an old man and a dog. When I asked who told him the story he laughed. 'A boy angel. He's in my head,' he said and tapped a spot just above his right ear. Just before he skipped off he said, 'An' when I get stuck on numbers he helps me.' The boy's mother looked embarrassed until I suggested that she write down the boys comments and not discourage his talking about what was a natural intuitive ability.

All too often, the 'voice within' sounds like someone in our life who was or is very critical. With time, their negative comments produce a recorded message that can be instantly played to feed insecurities that will confirm that we are stupid, ugly, fat, worthless, or any number of other destructive words said to diminish confidence and make the speaker feel superior.

We are also adept at creating an inner dialogue that occurs in times of doubts, indecision and debates on need versus want. We grab a candy bar instead of a piece of fruit, and battle with the inner demon who instantly recites all the reasons the choice was wrong. A new purse or the newest computer gadget gives instant gratification, but an inner dialog peppered with words that are insured to produce guilt tarnishes the gratification with a lecture on financial responsibility.

This inner dialog between what a person should do versus what they did can sound like their logical self doing battle with their bratty five–year-old self. The feedback may also come from years of programming other peoples' beliefs into our system. Accustomed to hearing personal thoughts, when the 'voice within' offers advice, a person is cautious or they do not believe the information given is coming from a higher source. Perhaps, that response is due to the 'voice within' sounding similar to the person's own voice. It is also possible the information mirrors the person's thoughts, so the comments are dismissed as nonsense.

As to who generates the 'voice within', the answer is determined by religious beliefs, and personal preference. God, spirit, guides, and angels, are the most common names given.

Clients and workshop attendee's have admitted that they taught themselves to ignore the 'voice within.' The most common reason for ignoring the inner voice was religious teachings. Comments about seeking attention, being possessed by the devil, or being mentally unstable, were also listed as reasons to pretend the 'voice within' does not exist.

Another reason for not sharing information received was that when the receiver got beyond the teasing and disbelief they asked questions to test the intuitive abilities. The general agreement was summed up by a man who said, 'if knowing the name of a person's first goldfish is the test that determines if I am a fraud or a psychic superman, I will let them stumble through a pile of manure before offering information that could make their life and choices easier.'

Choosing to share what is seen, sensed or heard, or keep silent is a choice that can be based on the situation or as a matter of personal choice. When the decision is to share, it is important to remember that not everyone is receptive.

Stories about censor and denial are common when talking to people who use their abilities, but few are as dramatic and heartbreaking as *Paul's, an office manager. He attended a workshop with his wife. She admitted she enrolled them in the class because she thought it was time her husband learned more about, 'the voice in his head.'

As a child, he had an invisible friend. Punished for lying and teased by an older sister, he stopped telling anyone about *Albert. At some point, the invisible friend stopped appearing, but through the 'voice within' Albert offered advice and gave Paul tidbits of information.

At fifteen, Paul tried to warn a friend about drag racing on a narrow curvy road. The boy laughed at the warning. Within twenty-four hours, the boy and two others died in a fiery crash.

Feeling that he should have done more to stop his friend and tired of censoring everything he said, Paul told his parents' and pastor about his intuitive abilities. Not only did they refuse to listen, he was sent to a counselor who was a member of their church.

After a short time on antidepressants, Paul started flushing the pills down the toilet and learned to subdue his emotions. Still, the sessions with the counselor and monthly prayer sessions continued until he left home to attend college.

Years later, his young daughter mentioned her invisible friends during a visit to Paul's parents. The grandparents scolded the girl and a heated discussion ensued. His parents' asked him to leave and since then have never spoken to Paul or met their other grandchildren.

Another reason people ignore the 'voice within' is disbelief. A vision is difficult to ignore. Smelling a skunk when living on the third floor of a downtown apartment and all the windows are closed, grabs the attention. Yet, without a harp and golden light to get a person's attention, an unobtrusive voice saying to check the air in the car's tires, or not eat the potato salad Aunt Midge made, is easily ignored.

No matter what the reason is for not acting on information received by a higher source, if the advice received becomes reality 'if only' regret sets in.

Not every personal message received is life threatening or even life altering, but sometimes listening to the 'voice within' can reap rewards that go far beyond the odds of coincidence.

*Carol moved from the East coast to Seattle, Washington to attend college and stayed in Seattle after graduating. With no family left in the town where she grew up, she lost touch with childhood friends and former classmates.

One morning, as she drove to a favorite drive-in coffee shop, her 'inner voice' kept repeating, 'stop at the donut shop.' Normally she ignored the inner chatter, but a feeling she could not define made her listen. Entering the donut shop, she and a woman almost collided. Carol's apology turned into a smothered grasp as she was embraced by the woman, who at one time had been her dearest childhood friend.

I do not believe in coincidence, but if you do, think about this, if the 'voice within' had not mentioned the donut shop, Carol would have driven past the shop without giving it a glance or thought.

For me, having a conversation with the 'voice within' is similar to having a chat with a good friend; one that knows my faults and puts up with me anyway. I cannot remember a time when I did not have this mental pest offering information, encouragement and 'what were you thinking,' opinions. Do I listen, always, but listening and accepting advice does not necessarily go hand-in-hand.

As for sharing information outside of work or with close friends, I still rely on 'what if you did this' suggestions, or 'have you thought about this,' comments that I started using as a teenager. I use that technique because it does not generate 'why did you say that,' questions. Also without knowing a person's beliefs, it eliminates the need to explain how I was guided to ask relevant questions that got the heart of the matter.

Personal Information

If it were possible to receive personal information that would eliminate emotionally polluted relationships, financial mistakes, and jobs from hell, everyone would spend nine hours a day meditating. Also, each morsel of information would be treated as if it were a life-and-death matter.

The reality is if a person listens, there is a flood of information that will help smooth the path and head the person in the right direction. With wants and needs not always the same, only the person can choose which nuggets of information will lead towards a goal and happiness.

As a sales representative for TY Inc., beanie mania was a first class education in obsessive behavior, greed, and adults acting like spoiled two-year-olds. One day, several adults confronted me outside an account. As I drove out of town, I heard, 'next time listen to me.' The scolding was a reminder that while exiting the freeway, the 'voice within' suggested calling the store. If I had done that, I would have parked in the alley and missed the angry mob wanting to lynch me.

During the drive to the next account, the three steps to wisdom, I offered at workshops was pushed into the conscious. The steps are; listen to what is said, acknowledge the information and thank the source. The process only takes seconds, but I was guilty of not following through with steps two and three. In fact, when told to call the store, I justified ignoring the suggestion because the cellphone was in my purse, and the purse was in the back seat.

Going a step further, I evaluated the intuitive information received about accounts, the company and management. Before entering an account, there was a sense or knowing about the general mood of the manager or owner. This always proved to be correct. Many times a store owner's financial situation or personal problems that affected the store were also given. This information was both a blessing and a curse.

During company conference calls, it was not uncommon for me to hear 'lie' or less flattering comments. At times, the motive behind the statements was also shared. Again, the information was both a blessing and a curse.

Going back to the idea of testing the accuracy of information received, I bought a spiral notebook and recorded the information given, even when it did not seem relevant. With time, I learned that when dealing with accounts, management, and corporate decisions that could change between heartbeats, the information shared was accurate. The why and, what were they thinking at the time, answers were seldom offered until after the fact. Any company change in policy that would affect me and choices I would be forced to make were never shared. This leads full circle to the belief that guides are here to help us learn and grow emotionally, but not pave the journey with a smooth ride.

My hypnotherapy clients also benefited from this exercise. I use intuition to help guide clients on their journey of discovery and healing. Paying closer attention to information given before a client arrived helped me prepare for their session.

Listening and using the information as a guide when interacting with a wide variety of people can be helpful. It can also be a hindrance when faced with personal situations that many people consider private and do not want to discuss. There is no magic answer as to when to share and when to stay quiet, but a good guide is if they do not mention a situation, keep silent.

A sober guide or angel, demanding submissiveness and rituals that involve candles and incense, as a token of appreciation is not my reality. Instead, imagine a telepathic conversation with someone who knows you well. Because of my attitude, what I hear is often punctuated with humor, dry wit and irony. My guides also has no qualms about saying 'told you so' if I'm foolish enough to doubt.

This is worth saying again; receiving answers to questions that will affect choices that need to be made, or lessons that need to be learned through experience will not happen. So, do not expect guidance on whether you should buy pricey tickets to a football game or put the money into the 'new car' piggy bank.

A twist to receiving information that will affect a person's life is a woman who had a lucid dream about her former husband dying of a heart attack. The dream showed how his death would make life easier for her and their two children. Instead of keeping silent, she chose to tell him. He said very little during the conversation, but he did say he would make an appointment for a physical. Shortly after that conversation, he died of a heart attack.

In reflection, she believed the lucid dream was meant to test her spiritual beliefs and teach a lesson in making a choice. Telling him about the dream gave him the opportunity to make an appointment, which he did, and he was told there were no health issues. Sharing the information also reinforced her acceptance of intuitive abilities. She was also quick to point out that telling him absolved her of any guilt she would have felt if she had kept quiet.

Impersonal questions are usually answered. As a sales representative, I spent most days driving long distances, so asking road conditions and short term weather reports became a morning habit. The information received was more accurate than weather reports, but timing was not always perfect and full disclosure is not a given.

During one road trip, an early winter storm dumped several inches of snow overnight. While sweeping snow off the car, I asked if the weather would improve and received a strong, 'yes.' Fifteen miles out of town, I drove into white-out conditions that made the freeway, the surrounding farmland and the sky look like one large cotton ball. The tail-lights of a semi-truck became my best friend. Ten miles from my destination the snowstorm abruptly stopped, and minutes later the sun peeked through clouds.

Did I word the question wrong? Probably, and I did not mince words at my displeasure. The answer received was to the point, 'be thankful, it got you on the road.' What the 'voice within' did not share was that the slow moving storm would intensify. Wind and blowing snow closed the roads for two days. The hour of stress was a better option than spending more nights in a hotel room.

During a workshop, I asked the participants about the tone of voice they heard when receiving information. The answers were as varied as the attendee's, but did not necessarily follow their ethnic background or gender. Everyone identified the voice as either male or female, and a few said there was a distinctive accent. While the inner voice was normally just a notch above a whisper, there were times when the tone changed to a command; a pointed warning that held urgency in the delivery. A retired military man said; in your face, drill sergeant sharp. A woman compared the manner of delivery to a slap on the back of the head to get her attention.

A friend shared that he only hears the 'voice within' at work when he is itching to make a sarcastic remark during meetings that, as he said, 'will be taken in the exact manner intended.' In the second just before he starts to speak he hears a sharp, 'don't.' For a long time he thought it was a carryover from childhood when his father would say 'don't' when he teased his younger brother. However, the 'voice within' was deeper than his father's voice, and the command had a sharper quality to the delivery. As a child, he learned that if the simple warning was ignored he would regret his actions. As an adult, he still trusted the warning for what it is—guidance to stay out of trouble.

For me, a command generates a why response. Learning to trust and react, without questioning the command, is a work in progress. However, when there is a hard edge to the command, reacting before questioning is an automatic reflex.

One night, storm clouds and a low lying fog gave new meaning to pitch-black. Less than a mile from home, the narrow road hugs a hillside on the west. On the east side, the asphalt curls over the embankment and is broken into chunks where the roadbed has washed down the hillside. Without warning, I hollered 'stop,' and my left hand slapped my husband in the chest. He hit the brake, and instinctively I hit the invisible panic brake on the passenger floorboard. Stopped, the fog rolled around us like a cocoon; visibility was barely two feet from the hood of the SUV.

"What was that about?" He asked far more calmly than we both felt.

"A deep male voice I have never heard before screamed, 'stop now'."

"He could have told me," He paused, but not because he was going to try to sell a lie that he would have listened to the 'voice within.' Directly in front of us, as if floating in a black hole, two eyes blinked. Seconds later, the massive head of a two thousand pound, Black Angus bull appeared. When the bull's chest brushed the hood of the SUV he gazed at us for several long seconds. Then he turned, ambled towards the hillside and faded from sight.

We joke that the bull spoke to me, but listening to the voice within, trusting that the information is for your highest good, and reacting to the information, are lessons worth learning.

Music

Music is audio; it is also intuitive. A violin can touch the core of our existence, played as a fiddle the same instrument will have us tapping our feet or wanting to dance. The beat of a drum can excite, and a piano can make us mellow and reflective.

No two gifts are identical, and no power will have the same impact on two individuals. Yet, ever-so-often a person is given a powerful gift that is like no other.

Marcey Hamm is not a musician. Even though she had classical piano for five years at a very young age, she did not pursue her piano studies due to the strict disciplines involved in the piano teachings. Marcey later fell in love with mathematics which led her to Nuclear Engineering, Software Development and Electronics.

In her words, here is her story.

"In January 1985, I was involved in a five car accident and died. That term today is called a Near Death Experience. The physical pain was almost unbearable from my car accident, but through the course of the following year, I searched every corner of possibility for help. This process came to a climax of healing and doors opening within me that set me out on a whole new journey. After my healing, I went into my self designed computer music studio for the first time since I had completed it the year before; three days before my car wreck. After turning on all my equipment, I suddenly felt very tired. I leaned back in my chair for a short nap.

"All of a sudden, I was out of my body, rushing through what seemed like a whirlwind of so much wind and motion. Then I was thrown out into this complete void of nothing - no sound, no light—just nothing. Soon afterward, these huge ocean waves of light and music came rushing all around me and through me. I was engulfed in this moment, which seemed like just a few minutes, but when I returned to my body, I looked at my clock—it was 8 hours later. Not only that, but my display panel was flashing with all these lights indicating something had been recorded. I put my computers into play mode, and this music came over my sound system. It was the same music I had just experienced out of my body. I sat in my chair for many hours crying like a baby. I called this music Inward Harmony, and it became the first of many musical journeys to come.

"I had recently joined a meditation class and thought this music would be perfect for meditation. I took the music to class, and the music was played during our meditation. We all enjoyed it very much. However, my friend, Leona, who was also in the class, had more in mind. She stopped me as I was leaving to go home after the meditation. She told me that I had to get this music out into the world. I truly thought my good friend had lost her brains. All I could say to her was that I was going home. I was not going to listen to her nonsense. Leona is the kind of person that once she gets something in her head, she doesn't let go of it until she gets resolve one way or the other with her idea.

"Every day after that evening of meditation, Leona, called me each day and sometimes more than once a day, to remind me that I had to get this music out into the world. By the third month of dealing with Leona, I had enough of her calls.

"I found a local manufacturing company and had cassettes made of my Inward Harmony composition. (In 1986, cassettes were the music format.) I thought this would get rid of Leona calling me. Boy was I wrong. Now Leona kept calling me about going public with the music. She said I could get a table and sell my music at these local fairs that are held in hotel ballrooms. I was so fed up with my friend by this time I was at my wits end with her phone calls.

"I finally got her to agree that if I went to a weekend fair and set up a table to sell my music on Saturday and Sunday that afterwards, she would leave me alone. When she agreed to this, I knew I was finally free of my friend calling me every day. However, I was going to have to do this public event. I can tell you this was not easy for me because I was very shy at that time in my life.

"However, I went to a public fair in Dallas to sell Inward Harmony. I had a table where people could come and listen to the music through headphones. I did the headphone thing because of the loud room noise. Anyway, my first customer was an older man. As soon as he put the headphones on and started listening to the music, he turned white as a sheet. I freaked out. I really thought my music was killing him. Just as I was about to call for security, he took the headphones off and walked away from my table. I sat down in shock, relieved that he didn't die, and then I wondered what happened.

"Thirty minutes later he returned to my table. He looked straight into my eyes and said to me, 'Young lady, seven years ago I was on the operating table undergoing open heart surgery. I was pronounced clinically dead for sixteen minutes, and this music is what I experienced while I was dead.'

"From that moment on, Inward Harmony has reached millions of people all over the world. Thousands of healing testimonials have been received. Even though scientists have tried to figure out why this music is so healing, they have not been successful. I always say you cannot put love in a test tube.

"One woman suffered second and third degree burns from a house fire. Within five days of listening to Inward Harmony, her doctors couldn't find a blemish anywhere on her body.

"A man who had lost most of his hearing working at an Air Force base regained all of his hearing within a year and a half. His wife played Inward Harmony for him each night while they slept.

"Another man was born with a speech defect; after listening to Inward Harmony for a few months, his speech became normal.

"A police officer was in an accident and was to be a paraplegic for the rest of his life. After listening to Inward Harmony for thirteen months, he was completely healed. No one can explain what happened.

"The stories continue on and on. Everyone will have their own unique experiences because all of us are Special and Unique.

"I can't explain my gift. I couldn't even if I wanted to. All I know is that I was given a gift of music when I died in that car wreck in 1985, and my life has never been the same since. There are no words that can measure the level of gratitude that I have for my dear friend Leona. She knew the music would be history."

Chapter 4

Aura

The aura is the life force, the energy that is generated within us. No doubt, someone has written a complicated theory that involves electricity, sound waves and a magic wand. I will rely on a simplified explanation. Think of the aura as a rainbow of colors that are generated by personality, health and emotions. Combined, the three are an expressive and impressive composite of the soul.

Several published books go into detail about the layers of the aura, the emotional and physical meanings for each layer, and the emotional, physical health associated with each color. The information is a good starting point, but how another person perceives emotional energy may very well be different from how you or I perceive the same energy, or what someone has presented in a book as fact.

Also, from what I have observed, people who see auras and use the intuitive ability daily do not seem concerned with which layer of color they are seeing. Instead, they use their intuitive abilities to interpret the emotions or health issues related to the colors they see.

For example; if concentrating on a person with a mental illness or strung out on drugs; my thoughts feel like they spin in a hundred different directions. Their aura is usually a blue-gray, but sometimes it is a darker gray, like a storm cloud. Someone else may perceive the color as poppy orange or neon green, or see the more traditionally accepted black as representing darkness and illness.

At an aura workshop, several people described a volunteer's aura as multiple layers of color that faded into each other and flowed around the person like a personal rainbow. Two people saw a blue halo surrounding the volunteer's body, but one said it was dark blue, and the second person saw pale blue.

While few people continually see auras as a backdrop or halo around a person or items, everyone is impacted by the energy transmitted by auras. It is a knowingness that is ingrained in the process of recognition and the fight, flight or freeze response to danger. There is no conscious awareness of processing the information or drawing a conclusion based on the energy.

These unconscious feelings have created an array of comments that are used daily as people are described as, green with envy, red with rage, mellow yellow, gray as death (illness), my true blue friend, he/she is blue (sad), or their soul is black as sin.

When a tree is cut it is believed to be dead, but that does not stop the wood from emitting an aura. A story about auras that intrigued me was a lumberman who watched the aura on a healthy tree change as he cut it down and hauled the logs to the mill. When the logs were cut into strips, the wood gave off a totally different aura, and the aura changed again when he fashioned the wood into a table.

Trinkets and old antiquities have been said to send out bad vibes or dark energy. Ask a person who collects antique shaving mugs why they choose one mug out of a dozen for sale and there is a good chance they will say, 'it makes me feel good,' or 'it called to me'.

Phrases about the impact of energy on our senses are common, and are said without a thought as to how the conclusion was made or why the comment fits the situation. These snap judgments are made within seconds of seeing a person or looking at an item.

If you do not believe that, find a place to sit where you can people watch. Without conscious thought, a sense or a gut feeling tells you the type of energy a person is transmitting; and body language and facial expressions add impact to the perception. Write down your first impression and then watch how the person interacts with others. Chances are your impression will fit their persona or come very close.

There are times when a person's energy and their body language do not coincide. The class clown, or the co-worker who is always telling jokes but never laughs, can make a person question the gut-feeling that something is wrong. A person who is acting withdrawn or aloof but is sending out energy filled with excitement or anticipation can make personal energy feel off balance. I observed this when a girl around ten years of age watched her sister being criticized for something out of her control. The younger girl acted like the situation was not impacting her, but her emotional anger seeped through the small room.

To see the aura, or at least the part that tells me a person's emotional state at the moment, I look just beyond a person's shoulder or head. What I see is a transparent color that shimmers off them like heat waves on an asphalt road. Like a heat wave the color fades, but the more intense the emotions that fuel the energy, the wider the band of color, but for me, the band is seldom more than two or three inches wide.

From my interpretation of that color, I can tell if my perception of the person is wrong (it happens) or if the person is acting a part to cover their true feelings.

The first time I saw a person's aura overpower a space and glow with an intensity that was startlingly and impressive, I was at a restaurant. *Jack, a dear friend, was explaining how he saw auras and what the different colors meant to him.

When the waitress set our food on the table, a woman was dissatisfied with her salad. Her complaints were rude, and as she lashed out anger elevated her voice. As this happened, I saw a blood red glow spread across the floor and up the walls. Jack kicked my shin and grinned like a boy being offered a second helping of ice cream.

The waitress handled the situation with grace, but as she carried the salad back to the kitchen, I watched the blood red glow that had bathed all of us change to bright Christmas red.

The glow around the table, floor, and the wall was extraordinary but what impressed me was seeing a different shade of red emerge as the waitress walked away. That difference was an impressive lesson on how there is more to an aura than a primary shade of red for anger that is the same for every person.

The energy within an aura might not nip a person's fingers with a 240 watt jolt of electricity, but that does not mean the energy in a room will not grab the attention in the same way a person's individual aura offers clues to their emotional state. Every day in subtle ways people use intuitive abilities to draw information from the energy surrounding them.

'I could feel the anger when I entered the room, you could cut the tension in the room with a knife, the air around her pulsed with energy, the room had a calming effect, there is a spirit about this place, this room is full of joy, the atmosphere was pleasant,' and 'I felt the room sigh with relief when they left,' are a small sampling of phrases that refer to the subtle ways aura energy affects us every day and how people automatically relate to the meanings.

A woman told me that she never heard her parents' argue. When they disagreed their politeness was chilling, and the entire house would vibrate with a coolness that crept into her bones. When the disagreement was resolved the atmosphere shifted. She likened it to the house sighing with relief.

The next time you want to impress someone or want to put someone at ease, remember that just as you are 'reading' a rooms occupants they are 'reading' your energy. If you walk into a room smiling, but your shoulders are slouched and your steps are slow, the smile will not compensate for the tired energy pouncing off your aura. The same is true if you are amused, and trying to make someone believe you are annoyed or angry.

Also, impeccable taste in clothing and a smile will not mask an aura steeped in anger, deception or depression. Nor will a dime store outfit dim confidence, sincerity, and inner happiness. If you doubt that, the next time you attend a party or business meeting pay attention to whom people gravitate towards after the initial meet and greet.

Most people have experienced the unease of having people abruptly stop a conversation when approached. Instinctively, the person knows they were talking about them. Facial expressions might be a clue, but without conscious thought the first impressions were received from the emotions vibrating through their auras.

At a workshop, a man shared this story. Arriving at a bar to meet his fiancé, he saw his best friend seated next to her. They were obviously deep into a discussion, but when he approached they fell silent. His first instinct was to demand an explanation. Instead, he kept silent and acted like he had not noticed their discomfort, but uncertainties caused him sleepless nights. A month later, a surprise bachelor party explained the conversation he had interrupted and several phone calls where the caller hung-up when he answered.

Another person said that one day when she arrived at work a conversation between a sly-as-a-fox female co-worker and an upper management male, abruptly stopped. There was a tension around the man, as if his was filled with anger but did not dare speak. A joke about them talking about her was met with stony silence from the man, and a smug smile from the woman.

Later that day, she was called into the supervisor's office. Accused of talking about a company project outside of the office, she was fired. She had no proof, but the previous weekend she had seen the female co-worker and a man who worked for a competitive company leave a party together.

Two identical situations where people read the presence of energy as awkward, but the reasons behind the feeling were generated by different emotions. How a person reacts to a situation, depends on their perception and personality. When working with intuitive energy, recognize that 'reading' the energy and interpreting the energy to make a judgment are important components of the act and react process.

With a slight twist to the intuitive senses, you meet a person for the first time, and they smile, and offer idle conversation. There is nothing about their demeanor or comments that are off-putting, but your internal reaction is not to trust the person. Body language can mask emotions. Because the aura is controlled in part by emotions, the energy inside the aura is the person's true emotions. When intuitively read, that energy lets people know that the person is not what they appear to be.

With minor alterations, *Sandy's story could be repeated by thousands of men and women.

Sandy was persuaded to attend a singles dance sponsored by a church. Her first impression of a gentleman at the dance was that his charm was an act to impress people. She tried to avoid him, but he pursued her. During the evening, several people assured her that he was a nice man who was highly regarded in the community.

Deciding her first reaction was caused by being in a situation outside her comfort zone, she agreed to meet him for dinner. The relationship was a Cinderella story until they married. The emotional undermining of her self-esteem and closing down her connections with friends and family started immediately. Years later, she was still mentally beating herself up for not trusting her first impression.

*Jack, the friend at the restaurant, saw auras around people and plants. With an Irish heritage, Jack was not the only family member with the intuitive ability to see vivid colors around people. Growing up, he and a sibling compared experiences and tested each other. That openness gave Jack a strong foundation for understanding what the different colors represented for him.

For Jack, auras were part of the scenery that he took for granted. Although auras were always visible, when he wanted to concentrate on the aura he squinted. For him, that brought the colors into focus and put objects and people into the background.

He saw three layers of color, or more precisely two layers of color and a series of black lines, and circles or spots.

The black lines marked surgeries, broken bones and other serious injuries. The black spots or circles indicated pain or illness. To prove his point, during a conversation he recited my health issues if he were reading a medical chart.

Jack divided the colors into two categories. Not knowing what colors Jack associated to each emotion, the following colors are generalizations.

Emotional colors were like a fog that changed according to the person's mood and health. If a person was calm, the aura would be blue. If startled, the emotional color would instantly change to yellow. If the aura was green as a person relaxed into a meditative state, the emotional color would change to violet or purple, and then to red if they were interrupted and became impatient.

The personality color was closest to the body. The main personality traits were a color that would vary in shades. For example, yellow orange, orange, orange-red—but the base color, orange, never changed. What changed the hue of the orange would be a shift in mindset—yellow orange for creativity, orange for energy or ready for adventure, orange red for confidence in what the person is doing.

Jack never used his intuitive abilities professionally. Instead, as a guest speaker for conferences, clubs and at workshops, he generously shared what he knew and taught people the basics of how to train the eye to see auras.

I'm going to share this because it is an amazing story of how physical and spiritual intuitive connections and universal energy work together.

Jack moved to another part of the state, and I lost the paper with his phone number. For several weeks, I sent telepathic pleas for him to call. Jack loved a practical joke. More than once, he called and fooled me by giving a fake name and asking questions about hypnosis or past life regression. One day a message on the answer machine sounded like Jack with a thick Irish accent. The name given was Mr. Kadiddlehopper, a name used in skits by comedian Red Skelton. This also made me believe the caller was Jack. The message sounded like it was being funneled through a long tunnel, and several words were unintelligible as they faded out. Caller ID did not register the call, and no number was left for a return call.

A month later, a new client, who saw an article I had written for a local paper, mentioned that her step-father had seen auras. I asked his name and, of course, it was Jack. His death and the message left on my answer machine happened the same week. Coincidence; I don't think so.

To simply say, Tracy Lee Nash sees and reads auras would be an understatement of the depth of her intuitive abilities. Within minutes of our first conversation she gave me a detailed description of my personality, strengths, and weaknesses, that was more accurate than any family member or friend could have recited.

Yes, I was impressed, but more importantly, her comments were a confirmation that when intuitive abilities are accepted and shared the powers can build into an extraordinary talent.

Tracy Lee is a certified research medium. Believing that continued education in all fields of intuitive abilities is important she has a bachelor degree in metaphysical studies and has studied psychology, Reiki, chakra energy, and crystal healing. She is also certified as a hospice patient support volunteer.

In her words, this is Tracey Lee's story.

"I grew up with parents who were extremely open and who did not censor anything I wanted to do. That flexibility and the freedom of choice allowed me to be who I am today.

"At five or six years old, I could see, feel, and hear things that the people around me could not see, feel, or hear. No one discouraged or encouraged me if I mentioned something I saw or felt, but it was many years later before I learned that most of the people in my family experienced intuitive abilities.

"We had a neighbor who read palms. During a visit to her home, when I was eight years old, she asked to see my hand. From the moment, she told me what the lines on my palm represented, it completely resonated with me. I remember feeling goose-bumps on my arms, and there was a shift inside my body.

"Needing to know how she could know personal things about me, just by looking at my hand, I spent a lot of time at the library reading books about palmistry and other supernatural topics. Slowly, through application and testing, I started to develop my abilities. I also started to receive messages for people who stood by me. Sometimes, the spirits were older male energies such as a father or grandfather. Other times it would a maternal figure or even a child who had passed away.

"At around age sixteen, I set up a backroom in my parents' house and started 'reading' professionally.

"When my second daughter suffered a seizure brought on by a very high fever and had to be hospitalized, my abilities as a medium became stronger. The doctors listed the tests they wanted to perform to determine what was wrong. The possible side-effects for the tests were scary. I did not want to risk my daughter's mental and physical health to the possible side-effects that the tests could cause, but I did not know what to do. I signed the necessary paperwork then went to the hospital chapel to pray. I made a promise to God to work for him in any capacity that he wanted if he would make my daughter whole. Nearly seventy-two hours later she was released from the hospital with no side effects from the tests.

"About three months later, I started seeing spirits as if they were three dimensional beings who could breathe. I could also talk to them, just like I can talk to someone in a room with me. Compared to what I had experienced previously, the new depth of understanding and communication was profound.

"During that same timeframe, I started receiving information about things when I was around people. I would be at the grocery store, a retail shop, the movie theater, even a park, and I would hear voices and / or see spirits asking me to deliver messages. It was fast, it was amazing, and a little freaky, to be honest. In the beginning, I had a very difficult time controlling my abilities, but ultimately learned how to turn them on and off.

"In 2007, during a miscarriage, I had a near death experience. While my spirit hovered above my body I saw myself lying on the floor in a fetal position. There was no pain or fear. Instead, I was engulfed in this beautiful feeling of love and peace. It was an astounding and incredible experience. I do not know how much time elapsed before I heard, 'It's not your time.' I knew the voice was God, and before I could reply I was snapped back into my body like a rubber-band snapping your wrist.

"Shortly after that I experienced another shift in my intuitive abilities.

"I have had always been able to see auras, the colors that surround a person and extend outward. After the near death experience, I began to see 3-D blocks of color that lay over the person. These blocks start a couple of inches below the top of a person's head and extend to about the naval. Depending on the person's personality, I will see one to three color blocks of different colors. If there is more than one block, the color of the top block will be the most dominate.

"I have named these blocks, personal vibration shades.

"In addition to the intuitive information I receive, the personal vibration shades tell me the person's emotional strengths, and what they are challenged with emotionally and physically. They also tell me where the emotions rest in their body, what that means for the person, how it can affect them, or stagnate their growth.

"Because I do not have to talk to a person, or even see them to know their personality and what they are struggling with, seeing the colors has made a huge difference in the way I work and the way that I can help people.

"One aspect of the color blocks is the empathic ability to sense sadness or pain in the particular part of the body where that person holds their emotions. It took about three years to figure out how to differentiate between their emotions and mine. Now, as soon as I share what I see I notice a shift and the empathic emotions I feel are gone. I believe that happens not only because I shared my insights, but by sharing the person feels better, so the energy shifts.

"It took five or six years to refine my ability to interpret the colors. Mostly, how I read a color is indicative to the emotion I feel attached to the color and where it is located. Even now, there are times I see a particular shade of a color that I've never seen before. When that happens, I stop and listen to what it means; how did my body feel when I saw the color? Was there a sense of heaviness, or was it light and fluid to indicate a positive response?

"The color blocks are the first intuitive skill I use when working with clients.

"A young man I'd worked with in the past made an appointment for a friend.

"Before the man and his friend arrived, I took time to clear my thoughts and concentrate on the friend, and the woman who wanted the 'reading'. While I focused, I wrote down what I was feeling; impressions, her feelings, what I believed to be the features of the woman I was to read for, and the personal vibrations color I saw.

"When they arrived, the woman looked very much as I'd expected. She was also very nervous. Sitting with her arms and legs crossed she was also emotionally shutdown. Because crossing the arms and legs blocks off energy, I asked her to uncross the arms and sit with both feet on the floor.

"I told *Cindy how I received my information and let her read the paper with my impressions. That way she knew I was not making up a story just to sound impressive. She agreed with everything I had written about her personality.

"I had also written down the letter D and written 'husband' next to the letter. She confirmed that was correct and confirmed that I'd correctly described his personality.

"At this point, I still had no idea why Cindy's friend brought her to me for a 'reading'.

"When I began to talk, I felt an ache in my chest, but my head also hurt. I told her that I saw her husband died very quickly from a heart attack, but also thought that he hit his head as he fell.

"She wanted to hear what I saw, but she had a difficult time with the experience and the information because she did not easily trust people. During the course of the 'reading' she started to relax and shared that her husband had been out of the country when he died suddenly from a heart attack.

"Because Cindy had not been able to say goodbye, she did not have closure. She had been asking him for a sign that he was alright.

"In my office, I sit facing a wall with my back to a window. Clients sit in chairs that face the window. I told her that he would send her a message, and in my mind's eye I saw a hummingbird, so I used that as an example.

"Her eyes shifted from me to the window and seconds later, as if her husband had choreographed the scene, a hummingbird hovered in front of the window. The hummingbird was the proof she needed that he could hear her and that life continues after physical death. As she said, a final, I love you.

"The depth of that session changed my life, but I was just the messenger; it was her husband and God who made the energy happen.

"Another client came to me with a list of questions but was not happy with my answers. In fact, she thought I was basing my answers on her body language, but that did not stop her from asking more questions.

"When *Mattie asked a question about her husband's work, I asked for his first name. With that, I was able to see his colors. At the same time, a male spirit arrived in the room.

"Her question was in reference to continued employment. What I received was confirmation that he was active at work and around the house. The problem I was shown was that he was not doing anything that was healthy for his body, particularly his upper extremities—his heart. I told her that a father figure had appeared, and he was telling me that heart disease ran in her husband's family, and her husband need to be careful.

"At that point, her skepticism vanished.

"She confirmed the heart disease and the fact that her father-in-law had died of a heart attack. As she spoke the spirit stood behind her nodding his head in agreement.

"A week later, she accompanied her husband to a doctor appointment. They did a stress test and found a blocked artery or valve.

"When the husband told the doctor Mattie had made the appointment after talking to a psychic, the doctor told them to thank me because without surgery he would have had a heart attack."

If I'm Crazy, I Am In Good Company

Chapter 5

Clairvoyant / Clairvoyance

Imagine a television or computer screen with no electrical cord to provide power. Someone asks a question (the question is not necessarily directed to you), and the screen, the one with no power source, flashes an image, or a thirty second movie, or a series of snapshots in black-and-white or color.

The screen can be a blank wall, the sky, a window, the floor; any spot with a clear view. When the image or mini-movie appears, sight narrows down to the vision and the surroundings and sounds fade into the background. That is my reality, and with only slight variations in descriptive words, it is the reality of everyone who shared their story for this book.

The scenes only last seconds, but for some people, once received the image or scene can be recalled. For me, that means that the scene will reappear as I describe what was shown. If the person asks questions the scene may appear, and sometimes reveal more information. Much like a dream, within minutes or a few hours, the information and images fade from the memory. If the vision is ignored the impressions and information fade quickly.

A vision is not a daydream. A daydream is a blend of hopes and fantasy. The fantasy can be woven into a novel, relieve stress, or with 'what if' thoughts and manipulation show an inventor how to create the first water powered automobile.

A vision is a recorded message or a snapshot. Through the process of explanations and questions, the vision might reveal more information, but the receiver cannot alter what they are shown. Although, it is not unusual for someone to ask the same question repeatedly in hopes of changing what they are told.

A neighbor wanted to move to sunny California to pursue a career as a personal assistant. She claimed not to believe in psychic mumbo-jumbo, but for weeks, in dozens of different ways, she asked when she would be hired for her dream job. Each time I saw a snapshot vision of a large A-frame house and horse pastures, close to a rugged mountain range. When I repeated what was shown, her response was always, 'not going to happen.'

When the dream job materialized, it included sunshine and travel. She was quick to point out my vision was wrong, and thus my intuitive abilities were a figment of my imagination. Then, shortly after being hired, her employer sold the beach house and moved to Montana. She still got to travel, but the view out her office window was steep mountains capped with snow, not white sand and surf.

Anyone who has watched a television program featuring a psychic will have heard words to the effect of, 'I see a baseball, I see a bright red dress, or I see a cat that reminds me of my Uncle Joe.' The medium is being shown images that have meaning for someone. Since these types of programs usually include an auditorium full of people, the medium's first job is to establish if the information has meaning to anyone in the room. Unfortunately, that process can make it sound like the medium is throwing out a suggestion and hoping that someone will pick up his lead and give them more information. Images like these also remind me of a children's game called, I spy because trying to interpret the meaning of the symbol can be as elusive as guessing what a person looked at five minutes ago.

The images do not tell a story. Instead, they are symbolic messages to be interpreted, which is where problems can arise. For me, a red dress could relate to work or a night out on the town. For the receiver, the dress could represent a person they know or the dress they wore to the senior prom. A man may think of his wife, a previous girlfriend or a woman he met at a bar.

During television programs where a medium is 'reading' for the audience, there is a good chance they will say something like—I see a blue ball that reminds me of my white cat named Angel. The clairvoyant may also ask a question like, I see a purple elephant; does that mean anything to you? The connection between a white cat named Angel and a blue ball is a personal connection, but it also a way to get strangers to think beyond the obvious.

What the medium received intuitively is a snapshot image, a symbol that needs to be interpreted. Perhaps, the cat named Angel reminds the person of their sister who is nicknamed Angel. The purple elephant may have been a Christmas gift from a favorite aunt. If so, there is confirmation and connection. From there, the psychic may or may not be given more information.

On a personal level, when thinking about an ice cream cone, you may envision a cone. Maybe the image includes details, like a waffle cone or a scoop of chocolate over a scoop of strawberry. Usually these symbolic visions are gone in a blink and are easily ignored or not consciously noticed. In the grocery store, a flash image of a bottle of milk appears while you walk down the cereal aisle, or you imagine the 'Got milk' billboard of a glass of milk and an Oreo cookie. Ignoring the image, the next morning you have no milk for cereal because the milk in the refrigerator has gone sour. Perhaps at that moment, you remember the incident in the grocery store and think next time you will pay attention.

A woman who used to insist that visions were 'witchcraft' kept seeing the image of a burning candle and kerosene lamp with a yellow halo around the glass chimney. After a week of having the same vision, an early winter storm broke tree limbs that took down power-lines. Without electricity for a week, candles and an antique oil lamp were the only source of light.

After that experience, she saw a car battery. Having just had the car serviced she ignored the warning. When the car's battery died, and she had to wait an hour for a towing service, she decided it was time to pay attention to the symbols shown in visions. She will ignore one vision, but if she sees a second vision that is similar to the first she pays attention. If she sees two visions that could relate to each other, like a washing machine and a puddle of water, she calls a repairman.

Another form of intuitive vision is shaped by memories. A person misplaces a favorite piece of jewelry. Each time they think about the item they visualize the piece and where it is located, but the image of a drawer is too vague, and an image of their father makes no sense. When they finally locate the ring tucked inside a small wooden box their father used for cufflinks, they wonder why they had not thought to look their first.

The news is quick to report on people who claimed that visions showed them the winning numbers to a lottery. I have also heard claims of bingo players picking their cards by 'seeing' winner written across a card. At a birthday party, a woman claimed that she saw the number of jelly beans in the jar before writing down her guess.

To test this, I closed my eyes, visualized numbers on a lottery ticket, and wrote the numbers down. When purchasing the lottery ticket, I let the machine randomly pick six numbers. The ticket and the vision had the numbers eleven, twenty-nine and thirty. Both papers showed nine as the Powerball. With four of the six numbers matching, I felt smug about the success of that part of the experiment. The following morning, not one number in the visualization or on the ticket, matched the winning combination.

I also dumped a bag of red beans in a jar and tried to visualize the number of beans. The answer I saw was five-eighty-nine. When the last bean was dumped back in the bag, it was number seven-sixty-three.

The test results confirmed what many believe; using intuitive powers for self gain does not work. However, if given the information without soliciting an answer, accept the information and use it appropriately.

Psychic Hotlines

The desire for answers, a direction, or even emotional support, siphons billions of dollars a year into psychic hotlines.

I have met two very intuitive people who have worked for a hotline for several years. Due to family pressure, working for a hotline allows them to use their abilities, yet conceal their identity.

However, the internet lists several pages of websites about hotline scams, so I decided to check out how they operate and include the findings here.

An internet search located several websites that rated psychic hotlines. From what was posted the ratings were the personal choices of the website owner, not the results of a survey or people writing about their experience.

Two websites, rated in the top five, allowed people to post a picture, write an inviting biography, and set up shop. Both of these companies charged a yearly fee and a percentage of the cost per minute for a 'reading' was paid to the companies for the privilege of posting with them.

I filled out the questioners for five top-rated hotlines that interviewed and tested potential employees. All five companies arranged interviews and asked for a short 'reading.' One business asked me to do short 'readings' for two people before the interview. The interviewers asked about my background, and asked questions that gave them a feel for how I received and used my abilities. The questions were general, and gave me the impression that the answers did not matter as much as whether or not I would expand on what I received or spin a tale around a thread of truth.

Each interviewer stressed the importance of keeping clients on the line as long as possible. Every company preferred 'readers' who use tarot cards, I-Ching, Runes, numerology, or astrology. When I told the interviewers that I did not use tools, all of them suggested learning the basic meaning of tarot cards to make it sound like I was using them. One interviewer mentioned that an employee, who used pickup sticks as a tool to focus their thoughts, had a large number of repeat callers. In other words, any tool that was used to keep the client on the line longer or call back, met their approval.

Companies that offered short, free 'readings' wanted the sessions to be strung out with chit-chat and vague tantalizing bits of information. The goal was to keep the client on the line, so they paid for the 'real' information.

Several times, twenty minutes was mentioned as a goal for the minimum time to keep a client on the phone. A stopwatch was recommended as a good way to keep track of the time. It was also expected that the psychics suggest the client callback in a few days or a week for an update. The consensus on how get a person to call back was to use a hook. A suggestion that the reader was receiving a vague image or an uneasy feeling that they felt certain would reveal more information later, was mentioned several times.

Salary was a sliding scale; the lowest one started at thirty cents a minute. Mind you, the client was being charged six dollars a minute. Pay levels were determined by the number of minutes accumulated by keeping clients on the phone. For example—one minute to sixty minutes, sixty minutes to two hundred minutes, two hundred minutes to five hundred minutes—represented different pay scales.

When asked what the company recommended if there was no connection with a client the comments ranged from give vague information until you get positive feedback and 'build' comments around that, to get them to state their concern and fake the 'reading'. Another ploy was to say the information was being kept from the receiver because they were not ready to hear the answer. Again, the call back in a few hours or the next day would be suggested.

Two companies monitored all calls. This was to insure that the psychic was following the rules and pushing the caller to call back. By the end of the first four weeks, the psychic was expected to produce at least five repeat callers within the same day as the original 'reading'. If they were unable to persuade people into making multiple calls in the same day, the earnings per minute decreased or the reader was fired.

Hopefully, I am not the only one who has questioned the ethics of the companies and the readers. But from the shocked response from an interviewer who could not believe I would turn down the opportunity to work for them, I might have been the first to express my opinion of their ethics and that of the psychics.

Premonition Visions

At times, a premonition vision is a straightforward vision that shows a future or past event.

While speaking to a sales clerk at a metaphysical shop, I had a vision that showed camouflage material being used as a bed for an Irish setter and a black kitten. When I shared what was shown in the vision, she smiled and nodded. She and her husband had just agreed to keep a daughter's animals while she was in Iraq on military duty. The down-to-earth vision confirmed an event that would soon happen. My willingness to share, gave her the opportunity to ask a more personal question.

One day at a restaurant, an image flashed against a blank wall as a waitress set drinks on the table. The image and information appeared each time the waitress passed by the table, so I decided to risk becoming part of the daily gossip. The next time she topped my coffee mug, I said something to the effect that she could think I was crazy, but her daughter would be okay, and eventually she would walk away from the situation. As happens, her daughter's situation had been weighing Jenerra down emotionally. What was unusual was Jenerra did not question the information and was visibly relieved by the message.

Since that day, we have had many long conversations. It took two years for the daughter to make a complete break from the situation, but during that time visions that confirmed better times ahead, helped Jenerra cope with the reality.

There are no set-in-stone rules on how information is received or how a person conducts a 'reading'.

There are clairvoyants who need to see a person to receive information. If a person receives information by psychometry, touching a personal object that would certainly be the case. Even without visually seeing auras, the auras energy will influence the information received. That could be another reason intuitive insights are only received when a person is present.

With cellphones becoming the primary choice of connecting with other people, receiving intuitive information during conversations is not unusual. In fact, without the distraction of auras, gestures, and facial expressions, the information may be more precise. Sharing what is received will depend on the relationship the person has with the caller. But, if a person was talking to their boss and had a vision of them being extra friendly with the owners wife; it would be best not to comment.

While reading e-mails from a friend who lives in England, I receive both visual and audio information for her concerns. At times, answering questions has been like raising another daughter, but without the need to remind them about piano practice or homework.

Many clairvoyants, including several interviewed for this book, are comfortable with what I call 'cold readings'. Knowing nothing about an individual who is requesting a 'reading' they go to their inner source, request information and relay the information received. This is no different from receiving information about a stranger in line at a grocery store, but it is not how I prefer to work.

Years ago, a woman made an appointment for a hypnotherapy session. Upon arrival she said, 'I don't want to be hypnotized, I want a 'reading'.' At that time I did not do 'readings' for anyone but friends, so I asked who gave her my name. She refused to tell me.

Sitting with her arms and legs crossed, she blocked her energy flow. I could not see her aura, but her stiff posture and the sour expression on her face, was as friendly as a rattlesnake ready to strike. When asked what she was concerned about she snapped, 'You tell me, you're the psychic.'

I declined the challenge, and ignored the sarcastic chatter from my 'voice within'. It took persistence to pry out this story. A friend of a friend told her I predicted a pregnancy hours after the fact. The prediction happened one morning at a restaurant. Shortly after arriving, my stomach became queasy, and I joked that it felt like morning sickness. Then a vision of me knitting appeared; something I tried to learn during my last pregnancy. When silently asking who was pregnant, I looked at both women and received two yes answers. Both women denied the possibility. One said a pregnancy test had been negative, and one claimed the timing was wrong. Both women were wrong.

My first experience with a psychic was a very talented woman who was highly recommended by several people. Curiosity and a lingering thought that it was time to move led me to her doorstep.

At the first 'reading,' all she asked was my full name and age. Her first comment was; 'You are psychic. When I am done with your 'reading' I have a question for you.' Sarah discussed my past as if she was reading a book. On current issues, she said, you are learning valuable lessons. The only insight she received about my future was that one day I would publicly acknowledge my intuitive abilities. Twenty-two years later, that prediction is coming true.

I visited Sarah several times, but not because I needed a reminder of past events, that were filed in my memory and hopefully never needed to be revisited.

Sarah understood what it was like to receive private information about strangers, co-workers and friends. Her advice on sharpening my abilities, setting boundaries on what information I was willing to receive, ethics, and using my abilities in a way that was comfortable for me, were valuable lessons.

When Sarah talked about my past, it was confirmation that she was attuned to me. But, a walk down memory lane about family, marriage, children, and dumb mistakes, did not offer answers or insight to present day dilemmas. Very likely, I needed to discover answers on my own, but hearing 'you are learning valuable lessons' was a non-answer; one that irritated me for days. That irritation helped shaped how I work with clients today.

In my experience, people make appointments because they are struggling with an inner demon. The devil on their shoulder may be a spouse, boss, parent, child, job or illness. They may long for a pregnancy that has not happened, or want to know if happy-ever-after is in their future. It could be that they are in the process of reinventing themselves or in emotional pain over a failed relationship. Whatever the reason for requesting a 'reading', a ray of hope to embrace in times of doubt and struggles, is a priceless gift.

For me, being asked a question opens the information source. Let me clarify that. Being asked a favorite color or what vegetable a person hates, are not good questions. Simone Browne, who shares her story in chapter nine, answers these, 'prove to me you are psychic' questions to put an end to the doubt. My approach is different, mainly because my 'voice within' has an attitude and a sense of humor. Faced with let's test the psychic questions, I hear comments like; 'Seriously, she forgot her favorite color?' Or, 'If this is multiple choice; I pick peas.' Since I repeat, word-for-word what I hear, reactions have been funny and defensive.

Clairvoyant 'readings' usually use all the senses. I cannot speak for how others convey the information received, but this is a close account of a conversation with my mother. She called late one night wanting me to play detective.

'I can't find the thermometer,' she said.

'It's in the medicine cabinet.' This very well could have been a reflex answer, as a thermometer had been in the medicine cabinet for as long as I remember.

'Not that one. I bought a digital thermometer that goes in the ear. It's in a box.'

'I'm being shown a box in the back of the linen closet.'

'I looked in the closet, it's not there.'

The vision did not waver. I see the linen closet with its stacks of towels and sheets. 'Look again; I see a box that is dark blue or black.'

For a few minutes I hear Jay Leno in the background. When she picks up the phone she says, 'It's not there.'

'My voice is saying, look under the pink towels.'

She sets down the phone and I listen to commercials. When she picks up the phone she says, 'It's not under the pink towels.'

'Mom, I'm being told you are pushing stuff aside. Remove the towels on the third shelf from the bottom.'

'The towels on that shelf are blue.'

'Remove the blue towels from the shelf. I see a pink towel behind them. Look under the towel.' While I wait Jay Leno executes a perfect punch line and the audience roars with laughter.

When she picks up the phone I hear, 'You were wrong; the box is black and blue. Thanks.' Then the line went dead.

Notice how I said whether I was seeing or hearing the information. That detail may not be necessary or even noticed, but I feel it is important for people to know how I am receiving the information given to them.

If shown a snapshot, I share every detail. Comments from the 'voice within' are repeated word-for-word, even when the comment does not make sense, or it sounds rude or sarcastic. The reason for non-censorship is simple; what may be sarcasm to me could be a family joke, and comments that make no sense to me could be very clear and packed with meaning to the receiver.

Some information is detail orientated, powerful and significant to current events in the person's life. At other times, the information is a calm reassurance that the person is headed in the right direction, or at least not rocking the boat to the point of capsizing. The reassuring information is not always received warmly, but life is a give and take rollercoaster. Different scenes and opportunities present themselves when necessary, which does not always correlate with current plans, ideas and wants.

Many clairvoyants and mediums can turn off the flow of information. Tracy Lee Nash, whose story is in chapter three, imagines a closed—open sign. When she does not want to be disrupted by spirits, she mentally turns the sign to read closed.

For me, just before a vision appears the room begins to fade, a blink will stop the process. Shutting down information about strangers can be advantageous, but sometimes the information being presented is for my benefit, not theirs. That being the case, even if I stop a vision, I listen to comments from the 'voice within'.

One day, a regional manager made reference to a recent discussion I'd had with a woman I recommended for a position. From the comments, it was obvious that the conversation had been distorted into remarks never said. Before a retort got me fired, a snapshot vision showed the two women stabbing me and another sales representative in the back with a green knife. At the same time my 'voice within' warned me to control my temper and tongue.

Silence was difficult, but the reward was a flow of information that helped deflate the other person's ability to manipulate situations. It was also a reminder that when the information given is used correctly, trust is established and the flow of information broadens.

When receiving a vision or audio information, logic would dictate that the information was for the person asking for information or a person within sight. That belief can lead to erroneous assumptions and confusion. That is why it is common to hear a clairvoyant ask; does that make sense? If the answer is negative, the information received could be for the person's spouse, child, relative or a friend.

Also, visions and audio information can be one hundred percent wrong. The theory is that the information given belongs to someone else. That could very well be true, but it is also possible the clairvoyant is tired or sick and is pushing themselves physically. All our senses are made up of energy.

When energy is depleted, it works like a short in a wire—intermittently and erratic. During a recent phone call, voices from another conversation bled through, allowing me to hear intermittent parts of a conversation between two women. Receiving information when sick or energy levels are low works the same way, allowing energy from several sources to mix together creating information that is totally inaccurate.

With insight and humor, David Tillman instantly puts people at ease. His interest in science fiction and history, a Bachelor of Arts in Theater, and his intuitive abilities to see the past, present and future, blend nicely in his career as a writer, producer and actor.

In his words, this is his story.

"It was my mom who first recognized my psychic abilities. When I was three or four, I would tell her that a person was calling, a minute or two later the phone would ring, and the person I mentioned would be the caller. At other times, I would tell her someone was coming to visit, and later that day they would arrive.

"Before I was five years of age, Mom started playing psychic games with me. She would hold a card up and ask me what card she was looking at, or we would play a game called Hüsker-Dü. The object of the game was to remember where tiles were and match them to the tile you choose. Instead, Mom would have me pick a tile and try to psychically pick where the matching tile was. So from a very early age, she was encouraging me to use my abilities.

"Mom gave me my first set of tarot cards when I was thirteen. For many years, I used them to give 'reading' to family and friends.

"Today, I seldom use the Tarot cards as they are intended. Occasionally, if a person asks specific questions, which can be more difficult to answer, I'll use a deck of regular playing cards. Shuffling them and flipping them over becomes a distraction, and helps me to stop over-thinking. From there the cards become an access point for me.

"Training your abilities is like working muscles at a gym. The more you work out the more positive the results. The hardest thing is not editing the information you receive. The minute I start thinking that something I receive is just me thinking, it turns out to be connected to the person.

"For me, the size of what I see helps indicate the timeframe. The larger the scene, or if I can feel the weight of the situation is on top of me, the closer the event. Although, what I feel and see could be the immediate past, because that would still have relevance for me.

"I started 'reading' professionally in 1999, before that I strictly read for friends or people at work.

"A friend who was desperately trying to get pregnant asked for a 'reading'. I saw her getting pregnant and having a son in a five cycle. It was early in the year, so a five cycle could mean, five weeks, months, five years, or May the fifth month of the year. It did not happen that year, but she didn't give up hope because I had been so adamant. She got pregnant the fifth month of the fifth year after I told her about her son.

"Another friend, who had two sons asked for a 'reading'. I told her and her husband that she was going to get pregnant, and have a daughter but they insisted that was not possible because the husband had recently had a vasectomy. *Bart's parents had died in a plane crash, and what I saw was so strong I told them that the daughter would be the soul of *Bart's deceased mother. They were adamant that it was not possible, but sure enough she became pregnant and the daughter was born on the deceased mother's birthday.

"A woman was in a relationship that was very abusive and she couldn't get out of it because she was in the cycle of abuse. I told her she needed to get out of the relationship, and that there was someone on the other side of the relationship for her. I saw someone from her past, come, like a knight in shining armor, and help her move away from the abuse. Because of the abuse she had lost her self-esteem. The lack of confidence made her feel that she wasn't worthy of anything beyond the abuse. But when I told her that she was worthy of having love that opened her up to the idea to try to move forward. Sure enough, she connected with a former boyfriend on Facebook. His encouragement gave her the strength to leave her abusive husband. Today she is married to the former boyfriend and very happy.

"During a 'reading' a woman told me she was planning a trip to Iran in late November to see her father who was ill. I told her that she needed to change her plans and make the trip immediately. She is a doctor, and changing her schedule would not be easy, but I saw the number four. I told her she needed to leave in four days or four weeks, but no later than that because her father was ready to pass. A month later I received an email from her. She made the trip two weeks after we spoke, and her father passed away four days after she arrived.

"This story is a little different but I think it illustrates that karma, and what we wish for, can play an important role in our life.

"I did a 'reading' for a woman in her early thirties. Her beauty was stunning, and her figure was perfect. She felt her beauty was a curse and hated that men talked to her breasts and women didn't like her because of her looks.

"During the 'reading', I explained that I saw a small dot on the underside of her breast that I felt was cancer. She took my advice and immediately scheduled an appointment with her doctor. When the doctor confirmed the cancer he said that without knowing where to look, they never would have seen it because the tumor was so tiny. Curious he asked how she knew where to tell them to look. He laughed and thought she was kidding when she said she had gone to a psychic.

"She decided to use metaphysical means for the cancer. The cancer is gone, but in her struggle to regain her health it took a toll on her physically and she is no longer a stunning beauty."

I have known Millie Gemondo for over twenty years. Raised in West Virginia, she is a feisty woman with a sense of humor. She is also a patient teacher. One night while we talked on the phone, I commented on the white tablecloth I saw on her dining room table. Laughing she told me it was not a tablecloth, the table was covered with stacks of papers from two organizations, that she was sorting.

Weeks later, Millie called and asked if I could locate an important document she had misplaced. I saw that the dining room table was still covered with papers and told her she needed to finish sorting the papers. The document would be found in the last stack. Millie made a game of picking different stacks to purge, but she could not outwit my prediction. The document was in the last stack.

Millie's degrees in English and Business Management led her to Washington DC where she was the correspondence supervisor for a Senator for many years. Returning to West Virginia, she still uses her management skills helping local organizations.

In Millie's words this is her story.

"As a child and teenager, when I went to town I would know that I would see a certain person. At home, I would know if someone was coming to visit. I don't remember sharing the information or if I did no one thought anything about the significance.

"I was in my twenties when after a particularly difficult day at work I fell asleep in a chair. I don't know how long I slept but I was awakened by a bright light coming through the living room window. When I tried to stand I had a difficult time walking, but I pushed myself to go to a neighbor's house to use her phone.

"I called a friend and told him to be careful because I'd had a dream and saw him in a terrible accident. He scoffed at the notion that a dream would tell the future but the next day, while he changed a flat tire, the jack slipped on the ice. The car bounced off the jack, and started to roll down the hill. Reluctantly, he admitted that if it had not been for my warning, the car would have run over him.

"Shortly after that, I moved to Washington DC. At a party held by a coworker, I jokingly told a man that I could 'read' his palm. Flirting with me, he offered his hand. My comments were so accurate that he accused me of talking to his mother. When I denied knowing his mother, he insisted I 'read' the palm of a friend his mother did not know. My accuracy was amazing, even to me.

"After that party, people started calling and asking me to 'read' for them. I would meet them in the park during our lunch hour and answer their questions if I could.

"I had no idea how to 'read' palms, but when I touched their hand a screen, like a television, would flash before my eyes. After awhile, I could get the same information without needing to touch their hand. If looking at them made them nervous' I shuffled a regular deck of playing cards to get their mind off of me. Now if the information I am receiving is not clear, I shuffle cards to help focus my concentration.

"One day, I told a person who lived in the same building where I lived that she needed to see a doctor immediately because she had breast cancer. She took my advice and the doctors found the cancer. Another time, I told her that I saw a man wearing bibbed overalls and holding a small red pipe was watching her. She smiled, and said her deceased father had always worn bibbed overalls and he smoked a red pipe.

"Years ago, I did a 'reading' for a Congressman. I advised him to stop the affair he was having with a younger woman who did not censor what she said. I told him that if he did not end the affair it would be public knowledge and hurt his career and his marriage. He did not deny the affair, but he also did not heed the advice. When what I saw came to pass, and his name made national news, I often wondered if he remembered my advice to run from her and not look back.

"One evening, at a political party, I met a woman from India who was offering 'readings' to fellow guests. When I asked her to 'read' for me, she refused. Instead, she asked me to 'read' for her because I had information she needed to hear. Frankly, I was surprised and flattered.

"During the 'reading' I saw her daughter was in danger, but would be rescued. A few days later, the daughter who was in Central America, was near the epicenter of an earthquake. Because of my 'reading', the mother was anxious to hear from her daughter, but not worried that she would be listed as dead.

"While working in Washington DC, I told a girlfriend that she was going to marry a man who had just entered our office. She laughed, and said, who is he, we have not met. I told her that he was a politician and she would stand by his side. Six months later they married, and forty odd years later she still supports his political career."

Nand Harjani's story is in chapter seven. Here he shares a story about a clairvoyant 'reading' he gave to a gentleman.

"Clairvoyant sessions are fun because they demand a plethora of gifts which include the ability to accurately 'see' not only a future event, a past (of this life) event, one or more past life time(s), the aura filed and some good conversation with the Guides and Angels of the person being 'read.'

"Take the case of Dave, a simple man with not many wants.

"Dave is a truck driver. His lot in life is to haul something from one place to another in his truck. Although he chose not to pursue a higher level of education his ideas and thoughts were very deep and could have just as well come from someone who took education to a higher level.

"Dave was a consistent man who had children, but was (at the time I met him) divorced for a number of years. He was introduced to my weekly meditation get-to-gathers, and began attending them diligently every week.

"After about a year plus into the weekly meditations, Dave informed me that he was ready for a clairvoyant session. When I asked him what information he was seeking, he said that he wanted to be with someone and perhaps even get married a second time. So all the information he wanted was who, where, when, how this would happen, and that if it was actually meant to happen.

"We sat down one day, and I began to 'tune in.' I first informed him why (other than the obvious reasons) his first marriage did not last. The details given about his former spouse, children and him were clear, specific and (according to his immediate feedback) 'actually quite accurate.'

"Having concluded what was behind him, the next many minutes began to present the various details he was seeking. Information flowed in such as: 'you will be sitting across from each other at a restaurant talking about your meal when you first meet her. She will be of such a height—she will have large brown eyes and wavy light brown hair—she will be very interested to hear you comment about your food because she loves to cook—you will like her pleasantness and caring nature—you will meet her in the early afternoon—you will meet her in XXX (the exact name of the city)—it appears to be a chance meeting as far as you are concerned—her name will be announced to you before you meet her—her first name is XXX (her exact name)—this will happen in about twelve months or so from now.' And more details as specific as the ones I have mentioned here.

"Dave being a simple, but deep thinking man felt that such a scenario was not likely given his line of work. In fact, he said 'he would feel rather awkward sitting down with a stranger and having a meal...and oh, by the way early afternoon? I drive for a living so how can that be?'

"About thirteen months later, on a weekday around four pm or so, I received a call from Dave. He was very excited as he began recounting an encounter he had just experienced. The experience seemed very familiar as though he had heard it in a story he had read. Then it dawned on him that he had just experienced in real life the contents of or session.

"So as the story goes, Dave had been hauling 'stuff' for a job, which had a deadline and took many day of non-stop driving to complete. On the last day, after having dropped of the last load very late in the morning, Dave decided to reward himself by buying himself a lunch for having completed his job within the deadline.

"As he drove down one street, he decided to follow his 'stomach' and as a simple person, stopped at the next restaurant he saw to eat because he was hungry.

"He parked right outside of Stella's Restaurant. The phrase underneath the name of the restaurant read 'simply a good home cooked culinary experience.' It was almost 1:45 pm as he entered the restaurant. The small room was a simply decorated quaint place. There was just one other table with customers, and it appeared that they had just finished eating and were paying their bill.

"His first impression was that the service was slow, and there seemed to be only one person holding down the fort. He patiently waited and subsequently ordered his meal. While waiting for his meal, he noticed that the woman who seated him was also the waitress, bus-person, and the cook.

"As he was almost done eating, the woman came to his table and wanted to know how his meal was. As such they began to talk. Since there were no other customers, she asked if she could sit down with him and ask a few more questions.

"As he sat across from her, he began to notice her brown eyes and hair. Before long, he learned that she was the owner of the restaurant and that both the cook and waitress were a no show. She explained that her passion was cooking, and her dream was to open a restaurant in her name.

"When he stood to leave, she also stood, and her height was confirmed. Before he left the Stella, he said he enjoyed both his meal and having someone to talk to. As he walked out, he realized when and where he had heard this before.

"In closing, he informed me that he had not only been eating at Stella's, but was experiencing other restaurants and more with Stella!"

Chapter 6

Dreams

To replenish the body's energy we spend one-third of our lives sleeping.

While we sleep, we step out of conscious reality and explore a timeless dimension where our soul has no restrictions and no judgment. At this level of consciousness, we do not question or doubt the intuitive powers that guide us as we talk to animals, visit another universe or watch a sunrise while standing on a beach we have never visited. It is only upon waking that a dream about flying like a bird, walking on water, communicating telepathically, or talking to loved ones who died years ago are questioned and labeled a fantasy.

The study of dreams is in its infancy, but it is believed there are five stages to sleep, with no set pattern or time limit for each stage.

The first stage of sleep is the twilight zone between full consciousness and sleep. It is at this stage of consciousness that a person meditates and, daydreams. There is a belief that it is at this stage of sleep that intuitive visions occur.

At the second stage of sleep, body temperatures decrease and the heart rate slows. Hypnosis, meditation, daydreams, and lucid dreams can be accessed at this stage. The person is aware of their surroundings, but the noises become part of the background and do not attract the person's attention unless something unusual happens.

This is similar to times when a person becomes engrossed in a book or a movie, to the exclusion of what is around them. They are awake, with eyes open, but they are fully engaged in the story—that is why when a bogeyman jumps out they are startled and their heart will race.

Stage three is the transformation period between light sleep and a deeper sleep. At this stage, hypnosis and meditation are powerful tools to inner awareness.

Stage four is a deep sleep, with no eye movement or muscle activity.

Stage five is where most dreams occur. At this stage, the person experiences rapid eye movement, increased brain waves, and voluntary muscles become paralyzed. It is believed this form of paralyzation is a mechanism to protect us from sleepwalking—acting out our dreams and possibly recreating a harmful situation.

One purpose of dreams is to help a person solve problems—intuitive information received by the higher realm of the conscious. That is not to say that every dream remembered or forgotten is packed with information to guide a person through the trials and tribulations of daily life. However, when dreams do offer information, they can guide a person through sticky situations or offer beneficial insights to future events.

Dreams can also be the inspiration that will guide a person to a creative pinnacle or direct a person in a direction not previously considered.

Paul McCartney has stated that the tune for *'Yesterday'* came to him in a dream.

Author Mary Shelley was inspired by a dream to write, *Frankenstein.*

Trying to find a cure for her hair loss, Madame C.J. Walker experimented with patented medicines. She said this about finding the cure. "He answered my prayer, for one night I had a dream, and in that dream a big, black man appeared to me and told me what to mix up in my hair…"

In 1964, golfer Jack Nicklaus had a dream where he saw himself holding his golf club in a new way. He credits that dream for showing him a different way to hold the club, which improved his golf game.

Novelist Stephen King has stated that story plots come to him in dreams.

The novelist Robert Louis Stevenson said this of his book *The Strange Case of Dr. Jekyll and Mr. Hyde*. "…and was conceived in a dream. For two days, I went about racking my brains for a plot of any sort; and on the second night, I dreamed the scene at the window, and a scene afterward split in two, in which Hyde, pursued for some crime, took the powder and underwent the change in the presence of his pursuers."

In sleep, the soul (subconscious) controls a person's thoughts. Thus the soul, the immortal part of us, that knows every nuance of a person's past, present and future, controls the dream.

Sigmund Freud believed that dreams are composed of wish fulfillment, manifest (obvious) content, and latent (underlying) meaning to the dreams content. The obvious is often unrealistic—a person can fly like Peter Pan, or the reward for exercising for an hour is toned muscles and sex appeal. The underlying content is what the dream is really trying to say. Flying could represent freedom or new heights of awareness. Exercise could mean that exercising the thumb on the remote to turn on the television, is not helping a person's waistline or their love life.

Freud's theory follows the premise that dreams offer a look into our unconscious—the soul memories that can solve a puzzle or reveal a past nightmare.

A person's 'voice within' or a trusted friend or respected advisor could offer answers and advice, and chances are they do. However, it is human nature for the logical conscious self to question the validity of the comments, or stubborn mule-headed pride could refuse to consider the information as factual.

Within a dream that could contain anything from baby dolls having a tea party, to a flight to another planet, information is presented in a way that the brain absorbs the information. That way, conscious personality traits that can cause an emotional train wreck, cannot challenge the content of the dream.

It is also possible that the reality being offered is bizarre or so beyond current reality that consciously a person would be unable to comprehend the information. Think of a farmer in the 1850's, and consider his reaction if told about a John Deere tractor, machines that pick corn and cotton, and circular sprinkler systems that can turn dry land into fertile fields of alfalfa. Emma McNutt, was the first female telephone operator, hired in the late 1870's. If told that one day people would carry telephones in a pocket and be able to call anywhere in the world in seconds, the statement would have sounded preposterous. In 1950, few people would have believed that microwave ovens, cellphones and laptop computers were possible, much less common household items in less than fifty years. Yet today, there are people who have never seen a rotary dial phone, used an oven instead of a microwave to bake a potato, or written a letter in longhand and mailed it to a friend or relative.

A dream stimulated by eating spicy pizza, drugs or alcohol may combine elements of fear and pleasure, but the probability of the dream revealing anything of importance are slim. But a dream about a device the size of a hearing aid that allows humans to be transported across town or to another continent, or an off planet station that control earth's weather may one day be written about in history books as dreams that became reality.

Dreams created by the soul and presented to the subconscious level of the mind deliver intuitive guidance. The information is designed to help resolve problems, answer concerns, and guide us through or around future problems or relationships.

Periodically the soul will offer a glimpse into the future, but it is not unusual for these dreams to be cloaked in symbolism and interpretation can be misleading.

While in her teens, a woman started having a recurring dream about nurturing three kittens. She interpreted the dream to mean that she would have three children, which turned into fact. What she had not understood from the dream was the children would be triplets, twin girls and a boy.

If you read the sensation grabbing tabloids that litter the checkout stands at grocery stores, you have seen the constant parade of catastrophe predictions. Many of the articles claim that the predictions are based on dreams from a well known psychic or a ninety year old grandma who is as trustworthy as a saint.

Seeing a ball of fire hitting the earth or freezing temperatures turning everyone into popsicles does not necessarily equate to a national disaster. Yet, jumping to headline sensation conclusions is less emotional than accepting that a potential love interest packs no heat, or that current actions are going to cause fire breathing reactions.

At the subconscious level, information is not censored or filtered through programmed beliefs and opinions. Dreams are interpreted, and the information is saved. Think of the subconscious as a giant filing cabinet that stores all the information you have seen or heard and every bump, bruise, lecture and praise ever received. Whether you remember the dream or not is irrelevant because the stored information will impact your conscious thoughts and actions.

When needed the information can be retrieved through meditation and hypnotherapy, or received through intuitive powers. This could include a gut instinct to be wary of someone, an audio warning, a snapshot vision or an overpowering sense to pay attention. Love at first sight may be attributed to having a glimpse of the future in a dream. Two people meet for the first time, but the circumstances and the feeling of knowing each other may be from a dream creating a sense of déjà vu.

Symbolic Dreams

Like visions, dreams can be shrouded in symbolic mystery. Dozens of books offer multiple choices about the hidden meanings behind a shiny red apple, a snake shedding its skin, or seeing your house burning. Looking for complicated answers can also say more about a person's personality than the dream.

Most of my dreams are lucid, meaning I know I am dreaming. Upon awakening, I might remember snippets, but seldom does a full dream make an imprint on the conscious. Still, what is remembered is written down.

Look for simple answers before twisting dreams into complicated manifestations of suspense and mystery. A realistic dream where a car raced down a steep hill and hit a stop sign, made me take a closer look at a business proposal. A dream where the devil ate my homework was funny until a week later when the computer crashed and the backup disks were contaminated.

In another dream, a church filled with smoke pushed me awake. A building on fire was the first thought, but in reviewing the dream, I realized there was no heat, fiery red glow or fear. At the time, the church services I attended were conducted by a very charismatic minister. New to the town, he was in the process of building a congregation and raising money to build a church. Investigating information I preferred not to question, uncovered the smoke screen the minister had built to cover lies and the theft of thousands of dollars.

The reasons behind my dreams were solved within days, but that is not always the case.

At a dream workshop, a woman shared this dream. She entered an unfamiliar house, with empty rooms and walls painted pure white. Reaching the end of a hallway, she turned and retraced her steps. Now each room was filled with inviting furniture and colorful artwork. At the time, the dream made no sense, but three years later she had to rebuild her life after moving to a town where she knew no one.

Elena Skyhawk, her story is in chapter nine, shared this story about intuitive dreams.

"In the first dream, I'm driving a car and fall asleep at the wheel. I knew the dream had meaning, but it made no sense.

"A few nights later, I had a dream where I fell asleep at work. Later in the same dream, I am at my mother's home. While my family is talking to me, I kept falling asleep. A sibling gets angry because I'm not paying attention, but each time they awaken me I insist I need to sleep before driving home. Instead of letting me sleep, they keep telling me the time to sleep is past; it is time for me to leave.

"The dreams and a similar intuitive vision made me realize that sleeping was a symbolic message that I was not doing what I should be doing. I was being told it was time to wake up, let go of the emotions that were holding me back and move forward."

Dreams about numbers can be symbolic and associated with events in your life. If there is no connection, studying numerology may reveal answers to the symbolism behind the numbers.

In numerology, eleven is a master number, meaning it does not get broken down to make the single digit number two. The meaning is intuition, spirituality, enlightenment.

After my father's death, a dream showed him sitting at a kitchen table drinking coffee. Behind him, a digital clock showed the time was 11:11. Since that dream, when checking the time, at least once each day it will be eleven minutes after the hour. For me, it is a simple 'Hi,' from my father that never fails to make me smile.

Research did not reveal who conducted the survey, but it is said that approximately eighty percent of people experience dreams in color. Unless a color is out of place, like orange grass or purple skin, or the color has a significant role in the dream, chances are the color holds no noteworthy meaning. Like the colors seen in auras, think about how the color makes you feel before accepting someone's interpretation.

A woman who liked to wear vibrant colors started having dreams where she wore only black. After reading that the color could mean illness and death, she jumped to the conclusion that she was ill. She did not see a doctor because she had this idea that if the illness was not named, she could prolong the prognosis, and certain death.

Several months passed, and she got a job offer that required a move to the East coast. In our last conversation, she laughed as she recalled walking into her first meeting and being the only person in the room not wearing a black suit.

Shapes like squares, circles, and triangles can also be symbolic, but the meanings are as varied as shades of blue. If an abstract artist or a quilter's dreams are filled with sharp angles and soft curves, the dream could be related to an artistic creation. But, unusual shapes, like a triangular ball, a bed shaped like a pyramid or a square tornado, are probably conveying a message.

Under hypnosis, a client talked about walking through a maze. When the session ended he said the square maze had been part of a recurring dream where he felt trapped. While hypnotized, he saw that the maze symbolized the precision of the path he had chosen. His actions were leading him to the center of the maze—success—without the frustration of reaching a dead end and having to backtrack.

Because items used regularly have meaning to the user, in a dream they can become a symbolic statement and intuitive message. A giant travel mug could represent travel, work, or a reminder to cut back on caffeine. A fishing pole could represent a vacation, or the need for time alone. A china cup, filled with hot tea and set next to a sugar cookie, could represent friendship and good conversation, or an important family event missed if working overtime. The symbols may be shown as stark images on a drab background, but more often they are details placed in a dream that standout. Perhaps because the item is out of place, the fishing pole is in bed with you, or the china cup is held by a gorilla, whatever the situation if you recall the dream the oddity can make the message more profound.

Imagine standing behind a rock sipping coffee from the mug you use at work. You feel safe and secure. Without warning the rock vaporizes and you face a tribe of angry warriors wearing face paint and business suits. They are holding fuel powered weed eaters. You wake up amused, and dismiss the dream as nonsense. Then within weeks the company where you work is sold. When the new management team arrives they are wearing identical pinstripe suits and their placid smiles mask a ruthless assault to weed out employees who do not meet their requirements. Every aspect of the dream had symbolic meanings that become reality.

A co-worker had elaborate dreams, and she spent a good part of the lunch hour describing them. I no longer remember the finer details, but one dream involved one of her sons.

In the dream, he was a magician who disappeared. His disappearance was factual; restless and angry at the world the son had left home shortly after high school graduation. A few postcards assured them he was alive, but they did not know where he lived.

In the dream, the magic act was followed by the son wearing a clowns costume as he walked down a hallway lined with mirrors that multiplied and distorted his image. At the end of the hallway, he stepped behind a curtain, when the curtain disappeared he was wearing a suit. Smiling, he waved.

A few weeks after that dream, they received a call from the son. He had been diagnosed as bipolar. He was on medicine, had a steady job, and was ready to connect with his family.

Premonition or Precognitive Dreams

For most people, precognitive or premonition dreams are personal in nature, rather than events that will become part of history and headline news. A common dream that is quickly verified is a dream that includes a person you have not seen in awhile. When you receive a call from them or unexpectedly run into them at a store the next day, the dream is remembered and perhaps, refusing to acknowledge the intuitive power of the dream, you chuckle over the coincidence.

Without mysterious symbolisms like talking rats, or atypical behavior like the ability to fly or walk on water, precognitive dreams progresses in a logical sequence of events that are plausible. Many of these dreams are so realistic that upon awakening it takes a moment to realize the dream was not reality.

Another common occurrence with a precognitive dream is that you are an observer, watching the event from above or from the sidelines. You can hear conversations, smell the scents associated with the scene and possibly empathically experience the emotions. What you cannot do is change what is happening or be an active participant in the dream.

If a person observes themselves in a scene, it is not unusual to have no emotional attachment to what is happening.

My belief is that the lack of emotion in a very emotional situation makes it possible to absorb the details.

Premonition dreams also give a person an opportunity to change an outcome. A dream about a car accident or an illness may be averted by driving a different route or having a physical checkup. There is also the possibility that no matter what the person does the situation cannot be averted and the dream was a way to prepare them for the inevitable.

There are documented statements by people who had dreams showing the sinking of the Titanic, the September 11, 2001 terrorist attack in New York, several deadly airline crashes, 8.0 or larger earthquakes in China, the Philippines, Turkey and Japan's 2011 earthquake and tsunami, just to name a few.

There are also filing drawers full of premonitions by well known clairvoyants, sweet old ladies with rouge tinted cheeks and blue tinted hair and tough as nail businessmen that never happened. While the dream may have felt like a warning it could have been nothing but a nightmare based on personal fears, wishful thinking, or a warning that the person took as secular instead of personal.

There is also another possibility. Time is only relevant to earth. The universe is not worried about missing dinner, or when to plant a crop, so there is no imposed timeframe on events. So it is possible, that events reported as happening on a certain day, a season, or within a certain year, like earthquakes, volcanic eruptions and floods will happen exactly as the dream presented the event—eventually.

It is stated in various books and internet sites that precognitive dreams of death are the most common. That would be difficult to prove, but a dream of death would make an impact and probably be remembered and repeated more often than a dream about marriage, divorce or an illness.

Three days before President Abraham Lincoln was assassinated, he told Ward Hill Lamon, a close friend, and several others about a dream. In Recollections of Abraham Lincoln 1847–1865 by Ward Hill Lamon, the author wrote about that day. Below is an excerpt from the book recalling what President Lincoln said.

"About ten days ago, I retired very late. I had been up waiting for important dispatches from the front. I could not have been long in bed when I fell into a slumber, for I was weary.

"I soon began to dream. There seemed to be a death-like stillness about me. Then I heard subdued sobs, as if a number of people were weeping.

"I thought I left my bed and wandered downstairs. There the silence was broken by the same pitiful sobbing, but the mourners were invisible. I went from room to room; no living person was in sight, but the same mournful sounds of distress met me as I passed along.

"It was light in all the rooms; every object was familiar to me; but where were all the people who were grieving as if their hearts would break? I was puzzled and alarmed. What could be the meaning of all this?

"Determined to find the cause of a state of things so mysterious and so shocking, I kept on until I arrived at the East Room, which I entered.

"There I met with a sickening surprise. Before me was a catafalque, on which rested a corpse wrapped in funeral vestments. Around it were stationed soldiers who were acting as guards; and there was a throng of people, some gazing mournfully upon the corpse whose face was covered, others weeping pitifully.

"'Who is dead in the White House?' I demanded of one of the soldiers

"The President," was his answer; "He was killed by an assassin!"

"Then came a loud burst of grief form the crowd, which awoke me from my dream. I slept no more that night; and although it was only a dream, I have been strangely annoyed by it ever since."

Few premonition dreams of death will affect a nation, but that does not make the dream any less important when connected to you or a loved one. A friend, who has visions and dreams about death, considers the power a curse; the sentiment is understandable.

While death and gloom premonitions make the news and sell tabloid papers, dreams that show happy events are seldom discussed.

In a dream, I was walking on grass. I do not remember seeing anything around me, but I stopped and turned. Behind me, my brother stood in front of his house; he held a baby wrapped in a pink baby quilt. His wife stood behind him. Looking over his shoulder, she was gazing at the baby. The dream felt so real that I called my mother to ask if anything had been said. She said no, but within a month the pregnancy was confirmed.

My track record for predicting the sex of a baby hovers at the one hundred percent mark for inaccuracy. When pressed, I repeat what I hear and tell the person that the smart approach would be to prepare for the opposite. However, the quilt in the dream was very distinct, and when I turned, the pink color was the first thing I saw.

The first visit to see my niece was when she was three days old. When ready to leave, my brother followed me outside; my sister-in-law was changing the baby's diaper. While cutting across the lawn to reach the car parked on the street, I turned to say something. My brother was holding my niece, who was wrapped in a pink quilt I had not seen in the house. My sister-in-law, standing on the step behind them, was looking at her daughter. If I could have taken a snapshot, and compared it to a snapshot of the dream, not one detail would have been different.

Another happy event was told to me by a woman who saw her daughter's wedding day. At the time of the dream, her husband had cancer and was not expected to live more than a few months. The daughter was attending college and had no plans to marry.

It would be easy to believe the dream was one of hope, but during the traditional father-daughter waltz she saw that the hand her husband held at her daughter's waist was prosthetic. When she told me how the dream became reality her eyes were glazed with tears.

At the subconscious level, wearing formal evening attire while talking to a pink elephant sitting on a giant white rose makes perfect sense. It is the conscious mind that cannot accept that the illogical dream is filled with helpful intuitive information. But when an unexpected wedding invitation arrives, and the ushers and bridesmaids are wearing pink and the bride's flowers are white roses, the promotion dream becomes reality.

Just as often as parable dreams are brushed aside as nonsense, factual dreams are ignored. A person not believing that they have intuitive powers and fear are contributing factors to the desire to ignore information, but the idea that a person is incapable of changing a situation also contributes to ignoring what is shown.

A woman on her honeymoon had a dream that her husband was cheating on her. Because her father's affairs and the subsequent divorce were strong influences in her life, she thought the dreams were based on old fears and insecurities. The dream occurred several times, but with no obvious cause to be concerned she attributed the trigger to the dream to be situations not related to her marriage.

Shortly after their third anniversary, her husband, recently promoted into management, introduced her to his new boss. She recognized the woman, as the same woman she had seen in a dream. She kept silent but watchful. Within months it was confirmed that the dream was a premonition. During the divorce, she learned that the first time he cheated was on their honeymoon.

At a workshop, a man shared that for years he had dreams where his sister was his mother. With the age difference between them, it was a possibility, but instead of asking, a gut instinct kept him quiet. After his parents' death, his sister told him the truth; raped by an uncle, she had gotten pregnant. His grandparents adopted him and moved to a different state so the family could live a life without censor from family members who were angry that their testimony sent the uncle to prison.

Accepting what is revealed in a dream as factual and acting on what is shown does not guarantee that the situation will change. I learned this in a dramatic lesson through a dream showing a house being burglarized by two adult males. On a trip at the time, I called a friend and asked if she would please check the house. She assured me that the doors and windows were locked. Less than twenty-four hours later, when I arrived home, the doors entering the garage and the house had been kicked in, and the ransacked rooms looked very similar to the dream.

If you have ever skipped pages or paragraphs when reading a book, and been forced to go back and read the full story because a vital clue was missed, you have experienced 'been here before' moments. Premonition dreams can produce that same déjà vu experience.

A business man attending a class shared that he regularly dreamt about meetings he would be attending. At some point during the meeting a conversation from the dream, would become reality. For fun, he had tried to change the outcome, but the scene always unfolded as if it had been recorded and he had hit instant replay.

I have heard several stories about people seeing death in a dream, but one that really impressed me happened to a neighbor who used her intuitive power to make a positive impact.

Lucy's husband had been dead several years. Her siblings were also gone, and she had never had children. Tall and slender, and with thick gray hair cut in a youthful style, her independence and attitude defied her eighty plus years of age. Her only concession to age was cataracts that limited her driving to the local market and church.

Lucy liked to serve a late afternoon tea. During that hour, she would fill my head with stories about life during the depression. She also spoke openly about visions and conversations with her deceased husband and a sister.

One day she asked if I could drive her to a town thirty minutes away. During the drive, she explained that she'd had a dream where she attended the woman's funeral. While sharing a pot of tea and cookies, she wanted to reminisce about their lifelong friendship before it was too late.

On the drive home, I mentioned the comment the woman made about a recent physical where a doctor said she was in good health. Lucy's smile was sad as she told me she never questioned or ignored dreams about funerals. They had prepared her for expected and unexpected deaths, and like that day, the dreams gave her the opportunity to make their last visit memorable.

Two days later, Lucy arrived at my house with a plate of cookies. Her friend had died peacefully in her sleep. Later she would help with funeral arrangements, but before that she wanted to sit and reminisce about the enjoyable afternoon where she had gotten to say goodbye.

Problem Solving

A crystal ball that answers questions, steers a person around problems, and offers a glimpse in the future sounds like a fairytale, but that is not necessarily true.

How often have you heard or said; let me sleep on it, or I am going to sleep on it before making a decision? The reasons behind the action are deeper than procrastination and the desire not to offer immediate answers.

Thomas Edison had a cot set up in his office. When a problem stumped him, he would lie on the cot and take a nap. He said the short trips into the subconscious helped him see problems more clearly.

Most people cannot take a nap in the middle of the day, but meditation can sort through and silence the mental clutter that makes concentration difficult. With a few minutes of time, nonessential thoughts are silenced, and it is easier to resolve problems or at least eliminate options that would not work.

Another way to use intuitive power to receive answers is to write down the question or concern on a blank piece of paper. Before falling asleep, read what was written and think about the question or problem as you fall asleep. In the morning, even if no dream is remembered, the solutions to the problem may be available. If not, repeat the process until you receive the answer or can decipher the message in a dream.

Recurring dreams may also hold hidden meanings. The fact that they are familiar dreams makes them memorable and noteworthy.

A friend shared a story about a recurring dream where she was isolated in a house with her young children. A wide grassy field surrounded the house, and past the grass was a thick forest. Although she never saw anyone, she knew that danger lurked in the forest. Determined to face the enemy hiding from her she would walk from window to window looking for movement from the enemy. That was all she ever remembered about the dream, but the dream occurred when she was faced with making difficult decisions. In the morning, she would feel rested and without any memory of thinking about the problem she would have her answer.

Starting in my teens, I had a dream where it is the night of high school graduation. When I stepped onto the podium to receive my diploma, the principle would say that I needed one more credit to graduate. I see myself going through a year of school and on graduation night, once again I am told I am one credit shy. I can feel frustration build as I head back to the classroom.

In the days following the dream, with no memory of receiving answers or support, facing the challenges was easier. The dream has not occurred in several years, but when seeking answers it is not unusual for me to see a vision of the dream and hear, 'there are no shortcuts.'

Recently, a woman overheard me talking about this book and shared this story.

*Stella owned a florist shop, and one day a couple entered the shop and offered to buy the business. Not interested in the offer she turned them down, but they left a business card and said if she changed her mind to give them a call.

In a dream, she saw herself standing in a meadow filled with flowers. She wore a black-and-white striped prison uniform, a ball and chain was clamped to one ankle, and her hands were tied behind her back. Feeling trapped she called out for help but no one answered.

The business was flourishing, and there was no reason to believe that would change. Yet, when she awoke, the conviction that she had to sell the business was so strong she made the call immediately. When the sale was final, the buyer offered her a part-time job at the shop.

Within a year of the sale, a grocery store, in the same strip mall, added a florist department. Directly across the street from the shop, a popular warehouse store started selling fresh cut flowers. With sales down and a substantial rent increase, the owners were forced to close the store. The new owners survived the financial loss by using the loss to offset profits from other businesses; a luxury the woman would not have had.

Obviously, dreams are not the only source of answers, but sometimes with and without a person's knowledge dreams work like a traffic cop and direct them towards the answer.

A woman who was sorting through her mother's estate was overwhelmed by the task. Taking a break she fell asleep on the couch, and dreamt of enjoying a nice dinner while sitting in front of the fireplace. After the meal, she sipped wine from her mother's holiday crystal and watched a movie on the large screen television.

When she awoke the sun was setting, and she decided to take a break and recreate the dream. In the movie, a couple visited an antique shop. The scene was insignificant, but it tugged at a memory of her mother saying that an old school friend owned an antique shop. A phone call and the cost of a plane ticket got her knowledgeable help and renewed a friendship.

Telepathic Dreams

An elderly gentleman in a nursing home told me that during World War I getting mail was slow, so he communicated with his mother by visiting her in dreams. He said that was how he learned about the passing of a grandparent and the birth of a sister's child. I do not know how he learned to use telepathic dreams, or if the ability was something he had always had, but for him the connection and communication was priceless.

During a telepathic dream, the person connects to the subconscious of another person. The communication may be verbal, the dream so detailed that it feels like both people were in the same room talking.

During a flight to Chicago, the woman sitting next to me was reading a book on near death experiences. The temptation to ask questions was strong and my willpower was weak!

She shared this story. When she was about ten years old, she had a dream where she floated above a road and watched a car accident happen. When the noise stopped she clearly heard her brother say that she needed to wake their parents' and tell them he was injured.

The parents' were not inclined to believe her until another brother awoke, repeated a similar story and said the brother was with their grandfather who had recently died.

The family arrived at the local hospital shortly after the ambulance and before the boy, who was in a coma, had been identified. When the boy regained consciousness he did not remember the conversation with his siblings, but he did have a message from the grandfather.

Parents talk about waking up from a sound sleep knowing they need to check on a child, and finding the child burning with fever. This type of telepathic dream is not usual, and is not limited to people in the same household.

A man I once worked with had not had a civil conversation with his father in years, but in a dream his father called him, was friendly and gave him a list of things he wanted done immediately. The dream disturbed *Ted, so he drove to his parents' home to check on them. Immediately, his father demanded to know if he had done the things mentioned in the dream. When the co-worker arrived at work, he was visibly shaken. He tried to joke about the twilight zone experience, but he never said he regretted following through with the gut feeling that the dream was more than just a dream.

Lucid Dreams

Aristotle wrote, 'when one is asleep there is something in consciousness which declares that what then presents itself is but a dream.'

A lucid dream is the point when conscious awareness tells you that climbing to the summit of Mount Everest, receiving guidance from the Dalai Lama, and then skiing down the steep rocky slope is a dream. There are several theories and 'this is fact' statements about the stage of sleep where lucid dreams occur. My thought is the stage of sleep is not as important as the communication between the conscious and unconscious mind.

During lucid dreams, many people can manipulate their movements and thoughts, or they can rerun a sequence of events and change the outcome of the dream. This type of reality, offers opportunities to experience different things, react differently to a situation, or test scenarios before making a decision. Think of it as hitting delete, and rewriting history until you are comfortable with the result.

In a loosely jointed way, this is what hypnotherapy clients do while working through personal issues that cannot be changed. At the soul level, the conscious and subconscious work together to change how negative memories control emotions, reactions and actions.

With a lucid dream, the same technique could apply. When a person recognizes that they are dreaming, they have the ability to manipulate the dream—like changing the details of a daydream. The difference is that when the soul level of awareness works with the conscious level of awareness, in a short period of time, profound emotional shifts can occur.

Manipulating dreams through the soul conscious is an intuitive power. Like changing a daydream, the process is not difficult, but it does take practice.

For example, during a dream you are extremely obese, and people are trying to force you to change your eating habits. The obesity may be factual, or it could be a parable for something in your life that is out of control. With conscious awareness that this is a dream, you can stop the action. Intuitively and perhaps telepathically, you rewind the dream to where you want to change your actions and recreate the dream. With practice, it is possible to create several endings. That would be like trying out five reactions to a tricky situation, and having the ability to choose the one that is the most comfortable fit for you.

Because lucid dreams are different from a bogeyman under the bed nightmare, or a dream where a person is a passenger in a car without a driver, lucid dreams tend to be remembered. Even if the dream is not remembered, the effect of taking control and changing the dream to give the dreamer control will influence the person on a conscious level.

*Pam's story is typical of the fear and overreaction people express when confronted with intuitive powers.

Pam had a lucid dream, where she watched smoke billowing out of the storage room of the dress shop where she worked. The dream was so realistic that she woke up shaking. At work, she shared the details of the dream with the owner of the shop and admitted that another dream had foretold a future event. She stressed that the dream showed an old lamp in the storage room shorted, and the sparks ignited a box of rags on the floor. The owner scoffed at the idea that dreams foresaw the future.

A few days later, the fire became reality. The fire department sited faulty wiring as the cause of the fire. Rags saturated with cleaning fluids and a can of lighter fluid quickly fueled the flames.

Several days later, Pam was fired.

The shop owner's reaction is not uncommon. Faced with the reality that a few minutes cleaning a room and an inexpensive new lamp might have prevented the fire, she removed the person whose presence would be a reminder that her reaction cost her time and money.

Notice I said might. The dream might have been a warning to Pam and not a notice that could prevent the fire.

The day of the fire, Pam was helping a customer when they heard a pop and a rush that sounded like a gust of wind. Turning, she saw smoke curling under the door to the storage room. Her first instinct was to try to put the fire out, but she remembered that in the dream, the fire started next to the door. With that image still vivid in her memory, she ushered the customers out of the store and called 911. If she had opened the door, there was a good chance that the fresh air would have fueled the flames, she could have been seriously injured, and the fire damage would have been more extensive.

Astral Travel

Another level of lucid dreams is astral travel—the ability for the soul to spiritually travel to another location. I am not sure if calling this intuitive power psychic spying is a joke, but it would make an interesting twist to a James Bond movie.

Let me be clear, intuitive powers should never be used to intentionally spy on anyone. Nor do I believe anyone should use intuitive powers to deliberately 'read' a person's private thoughts. Reality is that when people are upset and excited they transmit energy. Like a radio wave the energy filled thoughts and emotions are broadcast to a wide audience. Unlike a radio, there is no on/off switch that allows the transmitter or the recipient to shutdown the communication.

Before someone raps me on the knuckles with a disclaimer to that statement, let me clarify that. There are people who have trained themselves to contain their emotions, and there are people who can shield their energy from outside influences. But until intuitive powers are accepted as natural abilities, people who can control their energy are the minority of the population.

Like all intuitive abilities, there are opposing views about the ability to astral travel or have an out of body experience. I will not argue with the naysayers as they have convincing arguments. On the other hand, stories about astral travel also make a convincing argument.

It is believed that astral travel happens during stage four of sleep, when the body experiences voluntary paralysis. Yet, there are people who claim to astral travel during meditation, stage two of sleep, when the conscious is still aware of sounds and movement.

The theory is that astral travel is the opposite of sleepwalking. The Reticular Activating System (RAS), a part of the brainstem, has an important role in physiological process of sleep. The RAS is also responsible for the voluntary paralysis of muscles during stage four of sleep. When paralysis does not occur people act out their dreams—sleepwalking.

It is believed that with astral travel RAS is working properly, so the body is paralyzed, but the part of the brain controlling audio and visual sensations is wide-awake. The dream feeds the mind information that makes the person believe they are acting out the dream when, in fact, they have not left the bed. Teachers of astral travel claim that with practice, these short-lived dreams can be prolonged.

How people reach out to each other in sleep is unknown, and may always be as mysterious as the Loch Ness monster. However, energy does not sleep. It is possible, that the process of connecting your energy with the energy of someone you know would be similar to telepathic communication when awake.

As for having an unknown person connect with someone in a dream, I have never heard or read about anyone that claimed their dreams were being invaded by a psychic army of spies. That is not to say connecting with a stranger during a dream would be impossible. But logically for that to happen, there would need to be intent, and intention circles back to having knowledge of the person being stalked in a dream.

Gavin van Vuuren was born in Rhodesia, now known as Zimbabwe, with a mixed heritage of Dutch and English ancestry. He currently lives in Australia and uses his intuitive abilities and lucid dreams in a unique way.

In his words, this is his story.

"I started to become aware of something going on in my mind around the age of eight or ten years. I studied the planets and solar systems, more so than star systems as such, to differentiate from an astrological interest.

"I thought strongly that there was a 'key' to life as we know it, and thought perhaps that the 'key' was in the form of telepathy. I truly believed that if I found the 'key' to open my telepathic side, I would enter a whole new world of excitement and joy. I would then know everything there is to know about life on Earth.

"Only one person I confided in actually got what I was on about. That was an uncle on my mother's side. He seemed to understand where I was coming from as he also believed in the esoteric side.

"After a couple of years, the studies waned as I got more involved in school work and the mundane things in life. As a young man I was angry, and looking back, I feel it was frustration on my part, having not found the 'key.' I took up martial arts to calm my temper, practiced it for twelve years, and eventually ran my own school. The discipline and freedom of expression really helped my self-esteem. I became a new person, with little or no trace of the temper seen in my earlier years.

"I touched on esoteric arts in different forms until I met my soul mate in 1978. She helped me remember what I always knew was inside of me. After thirty-odd years, I came to understand that I have always been a healer and teacher and that belief grows stronger every day.

"In one form or another, I have been teaching for over twenty years. Using martial arts, computers and esoteric arts, I have helped people heal themselves. In the last five years or so, I discovered that healing is my real passion. I consider myself a healer, illuminator and teacher.

"What I do is really complex, yet incredibly simple. Broadly speaking, I use an alchemic brew of healing modalities such as Reiki and Shamanic healing, spiced with intuition and guidance from my Guides and Angels, to channel healing energy to where it can perform what it needs to perform. I also use intuition and guidance from my Guides and Angels, and other ethereal helpers, to teach and enlighten people to help them achieve their own awareness of the spiritual world.

"I see things differently from the way others do—I guess we all do. I do not do things strictly by the book—never have. I believe that when you work to the letter of the 'law,' or exactly the way things are taught, you put restrictions on your own style, and what you can achieve if you would only allow your creative self to come to the fore.

"My soul-mate and wife of nearly thirty years was the starting point of my awareness and enlightenment. I started exploring astral traveling in the late 1990's. Lifting myself out of my body, I would look around the room for a while, enjoying the experiences—although they were few and far between; being unpracticed, and new to astral traveling.

"Before I migrated to Australia, I contacted my brother who lived in Brisbane at the time, and asked if he would help me in an experiment. He was not enlightened at all, so using the word 'experiment' was the way to go. I said I was able to astral travel and wanted to travel to his home. At the time I had not seen the house in person or in photos. I would look around his home and then tell him what I had seen. His job was to validate my experience.

"Well, I did travel to his home, and found myself in a garage, with a workbench against the far wall. The main garage door was closed, but a door next to the workbench was open and led to the house. I also identified a bucket, and some items on the workbench.

"When I phoned my brother soon after this event, he validated everything I'd seen, even down to colors on the walls and the color of the bucket.

"A few years ago, I joined a few groups on the internet at different esoteric websites. I offered my services to help people who seemed to be in trouble, or who just wanted to make sense of what was happening in their lives.

"With their permission, I astral traveled to their homes, had a look around, and fed back my feelings on what was going on.

"On one, occasion, I traveled to a lady's home in England. She lived in one of the typical homes you see on television, semi-detached, two or three story homes, with a narrow entrance, a staircase on the left, and pictures hung in the short hallway on the right.

"I looked into a room near the staircase and saw a man sitting at a small round table. He was wearing shorts and a singlet. He was smoking a cigarette and playing cards on his own. I knew he was not part of this lady's family; more like a family friend, or friend of her father's. He was unshaven and slovenly looking. I did not see auras at the time, but I definitely felt them. His aura told me that he was a negative energy, and what specifically entered my mind was that he was a sex offender. The man was bad news!

"I looked into the other rooms and saw old fashioned lounge furniture in a larger room. Another room appeared to be some sort of office. There was no other energy in the house that offended me.

"I told the lady everything I saw, I felt she would want to know all the details, no matter what they were. She commented that she had always been afraid of that man, but did not elaborate whether there had been any events that substantiated her comments.

"On another occasion, a lady told me that she felt someone had been watching her. I used astral travel, and arrived at the lady's house on a dark night, that felt full of foreboding.

"Entering the house it was dark, but not so dark that I couldn't see my way around, or maybe that was inner vision. On the first landing, there was a roof or ceiling that opened to the outside. It had been breached as if by a lightning strike; it was broken and looked torn. I looked outside, and saw a man standing across the road. He stood just out of the reach of the streetlight, but I could see him quite clearly. He wore a greenish-brown jacket, with the collar turned up, and his long scraggly looking hair hung over his jacket collar.

"Clearly, he was watching the lady's building. He was the only person across the road, and behind him was empty land. Also, there was no bus stop. I felt he was watching the pattern of the tenants for reasons that were not good. I told the lady what I had seen, and she asked me what she could do about it. I told her to make sure her doors were secure, and locked, and not to open the door to anyone that night. I also suggested she call the police to have them send someone to check on her.

"I have had really good results with using healing energy to help people locally and overseas. Recently, I conducted a trial of a new method of energy healing I had learned. Using my Facebook page to reach out to the world, I asked for volunteers.

"One volunteer was a lady from Canada who had been having immense pain in her back, to the point where she was visiting a chiropractor several times a week. She was also on pain medication several times each day. After the first (remote) healing session, she commented on a significant improvement in her pain relief. By the second session, she told me that she had been able to reduce her pain medication to one dose per day, and she had seen her chiropractor only once in over a week."

If I'm Crazy, I Am In Good Company

Chapter 7

Empathy

Neuroscientists have identified an 'empathy circuit' in the same region of the brain that processes personal experiences, like burning a finger on a hot stove or losing a beloved pet. When a person shares an experience, the listener can emotionally or physically relates to, the listener taps into the memory. Then from the perspective of the other person, the listener feels empathy for the person and the situation.

I mention the neuroscientist's explanation of empathy because empathy created by memories or the heart tug of an emotional moment, and intuitive empathy, differ. With intuitive empathy, a person has the ability to sense or feel a person's physically pain and their emotions—no previous experience to draw upon is necessary.

The level of empathic awareness differs from person-to-person, and the situation will play a part in the depth of their awareness. However, empathic connections happen to everyone periodically. A good example of this is fiction and non-fiction books and movies about war, the holocaust, betrayal, terminal illness, and lost love. One reason these stories are popular is because the drama connects to a person's empathy. Tears of joy and sorrow are mixed with the desire to see the characters triumph. But at the same time, it is not necessary for the reader/viewer to have personally experienced a similar situation to be emotionally affected by the story.

The same is true in daily life. When a person talks about an emotionally charged situation, feeling empathy for their situation is not unusual. What makes intuitive empathy different than empathy is the depth of the emotions experienced, and how long the emotions affect the listener.

The most difficult aspect of an intuitive empath is not accepting another person's emotional trauma as theirs. For example, a friend is going through a rough time with a relationship. Whether it is a divorce or don't call me again split, you can relate to the person's feelings of betrayal and loss. If their situation starts to affect your personal relationship, you have taken ownership of their emotions. Another example would be allowing someone's financial situation to make you start worrying about money, even though your finances are stable.

The ability for an empath to nurture and not become emotionally entangled in the drama, is a balancing act that needs to be learned. Not only for the intuitive person's mental health but because taking on someone else's battle does not help them learn a lesson. Also becoming an enabler (making excuses for a person's actions) stunts the emotional and spiritual growth of both parties.

An intuitive empathic can also be an easy target for what I call an emotional vampire. These individuals care about one person—themselves. They turn all conversations towards their feelings, beliefs, and problems. Instead of needing blood to sustain life, these individuals feed off the intuitive person's energy and sympathy.

Typically, the empath feeds the vampires need for reassurance and strokes their ego with words of encouragement, but during the process, the vampire drains the empathic person's reservoir of energy dry. If the empath tries to inject personal concerns into the conversation, the emotional vampire cuts them off or leaves. That leaves the empath to deal with their raw emotions, lack of physical energy, and the emotions of the vampire, without any support.

At work, an emotional vampire will use stories to create sympathy. I have seen managers use those stores to justify a person's lack of work ethics and to dump the vampires work onto the desks of reliable workers.

Several years ago, a man called me about past life regression. Due to where he lived, an appointment was not possible. During the conversation, *Andrew said he was emotionally and physically depleted, but swore nothing in his life was out of balance. That was why he wanted to explore past life regression.

After a few probing questions, he admitted that he was worried about his brother who was holding onto anger from a traumatic divorce. The brother called him regularly to tell him all the injustices that happened to him at work, with girlfriends and anyone who dared to cross his path. By the end of the conversation, Andrew would be offering the brother money to help tide him over till payday—the money was never repaid. On a regular basis, he also offered to run interference with their father, and smooth things over with a colleague at the construction company where they both worked.

I gave him the definition of an intuitive empathic and an emotional vampire, and asked if he knew anyone who qualified. He had a good sense of humor and we talked about setting boundaries. Several months later, he called to say he felt healthy, he no longer had trouble sleeping, and his bank balance was at an all time high.

When a person changes their actions, it is not unusual for the receiver to react negatively. In this case, when the personal financial loans were terminated, and Andrew forced the brother to handle his own emotional dramas, the brother became angry. At the time of our second conversation, the brother was still not speaking to Andrew. However, Andrew's father had assured him that the brother was learning to take care of his own problems.

If stuck in a slow moving line, the sound and sight of a baby laughing relieves stress and impatience, for everyone but a hard core sourpuss. Husbands have claimed to feel contractions while wives are in labor. If someone catches a finger in a door, instinctively observers of the situation will curl their fingers and wince as phantom pain triggers the reaction. Empathic senses also trigger tears over sad stories or a touching homecoming, and a blush or discomfort when witnessing a person's embarrassment.

It is easier to associate empathic responses to people emotionally connected to us or a tear jerking scene. However, with intuitive empathy it is not unusual to feel the pain, fear, joy or stress attached to the energy generated from auras.

Imagine enjoying a meal in a restaurant with good friends. The conversation is pleasant, and you are in a mellow mood. Without warning or cause, a sharp pain grips your knee or it feels like a vice is tightening around your skull. You look around the room and spot a mother cleaning blood off a child's scrapped knee, or you see a man rubbing the back of his neck to ease a headache. When the source of the emotions is identified, the pain you feel disappears. These are not unrealistic experiences for an intuitive empath.

Consider the ability to sense Mr. I'Know-it-all's mood by facial expressions, and body language. Let's assume the person is angry at the world, you in particular; that is more fun and problematic.

The first impression of his mood may hit you at the gut level. The gut twists, the stomach aches, butterflies take flight, and those signals may make you a little lightheaded or leave a sour taste in your mouth.

If your reaction is at heart level, a band squeezes the rib cage, tightening the chest and making it difficult to breathe. The heart flutters and kicks into overdrive. When the breath constricts, it feels like the heart skips a beat.

At the conscious level, all the emotions register. The fight, flight, or freeze instinct of self preservation kicks in as you consider your options.

If you have empathic intuitive powers the process goes a step further because the information being received can affect you emotionally, physically, or both.

Say you and Mr. I'Know-it-all are feeling similar emotions; tight chest, shallow breathing, and tenses muscles. Your emotions are alert but clear. His emotions are clouded with righteous anger, confrontational and erratic.

Being empathic, his emotions mix with your emotions. Until you separate his emotions from yours, the result is confusion that can cloud your judgment and reactions.

That dramatization might sound like a farfetched fantasy, but when faced with anger it is not an unfeasible situation to encounter, and the entire process happens in seconds.

Unless you are in total denial or have a Fairy Godmother who wipes out all bad memories; a stubbed toe has made you teary-eyed, you have burnt a finger on a match, been sick enough to think death was a healthy alternative, and had a physical or verbally abusive relationship with a family member, friend or a sweet talking charmer who turned into an ugly soul eating toad. So, at the conscious level of awareness you understand pain, loss and betrayal.

At the subconscious level, the emotional impact to divorce, betrayal, death, loss of a job or home, or a severe illness are stored as memories. On the positive end of the scale, marriage, a child's birth, a job promotion, love, and achieving a goal, also leave emotional impressions that are never forgotten.

When someone shares happy or traumatic news or the local news channel is broadcasting pictures of the latest horror story, you sympathize with the people on an emotional level. If you have gone through a similar experience the emotions may be more profound, but even without a memory that correlates to what the person is experiencing, do not discount intuitive empathic power as nonsense or superficial.

It is also possible for empathic energy to influence the emotional state of another person or a room full of people. Simply by entering a room, charismatic ministers, and some motivational speakers and politicians can change the atmosphere of a room. Using empathic powers to transmit positive energy, these individuals can uplift spirits, and induce powerful emotions that sway people to join their crusade and donate millions of dollar.

On a more personal level, an example would be encountering a person on an emotional rollercoaster of fear, stress and anger. In a soothing voice, you talk to them. From a subconscious level, your empathic powers send calming energy through the tone of your voice and your aura energy. The two actions work together, and although the situation has not changed, through the use of basic empathic skills the person calms down.

The opposite could also happen. Say you are upset about something at work. Without saying a word, your emotions simmer. Some people will sense the change in your aura and steer clear of you, but some people will be affected by the negative energy you emit and their mood will shift without having any idea of why.

When you are the receiver of this type of emotional energy, it is possible to lose sight of the fact that the emotions are not owned by you. Mind you, no one is immune to emotional mood swings, but long term association with people who consistently transmit energy filled with negative undercurrents can affect emotional and physical health.

While talking to a neighbor, who was on oxygen, my chest began to ache. My breathing was fine, but it felt like my chest was weighted down with bricks; making it impossible for my lungs to fill with air. Asking the woman how she felt got an, 'I'm fine' answer. As we continued to talk, my breathing felt (in reality it did not change) more labored.

My phantom symptoms usually disappear as soon as I ask a, 'do you have a headache?' or 'does you back hurt?' type of question. The fact that my lungs continued to feel like I was gasping for breath, was a concern. My 'voice within' urged me to push the point.

Rather than walk around the issue I told her I was psychic. Yes, I used the hated word because it covers a multitude of sins and grabs a person's attention. I told her how I felt, and that she needed to see a doctor immediately. She did not sneer or laugh, but she certainly was not impressed. Nor did she budge on her stance that her lungs were fine, and a doctor appointment two days later was soon enough to confirm that fact.

I waited for a call after the appointment—it never came. A week later the suspense reached a peak and I called her. Apparently the doctors, 'Your lungs sound funny. You need to be in the hospital,' did not impress her either. Several weeks later, another doctor ordered tests. She had lost fifty percent use of both lungs.

Each year, Millie Gemondo, her story is in chapter five, and I give each other a New Years 'reading'. The 'readings' are more fun than a New Year's resolution, and at times more productive.

One year, I told Millie she needed to go to the doctor before her cold turned into bronchitis. Her response was 'what cold?' That was a Friday evening. On Sunday, she called to say the prediction had turned into a curse. Because it was a holiday weekend, her doctor advised her to stay warm, and come to the office on Monday. Monday she was admitted to the hospital for bronchial pneumonia.

Becoming a hypochondriac over aches and pains associated to another person's symptoms is pointless. Carrying emotional baggage empathically received is also pointless. How a person decides to use the ability is personal but with acceptance comes knowledge and it could change the situation or even affect your wellbeing—your choice.

Sensitivity to continual noise and a desire not to be exposed to large crowds are traits of intuitive empathy.

Imagine being at a ballgame or an amusement park. Between auras, and continual high levels of noise from speakers and people, your body and emotions are on overload, much like a sugar high. After a period of time, most people will find the overload physically draining. If you are open to empathic energy the overload can be mentally and physically overpowering.

That is why it is not unusual for people to need a day to recoup after spending time in large crowds or even at a party where one or two high energy individuals dominate the conversation, and control the flow of energy through their actions.

The main point to remember about intuitive empathy is to only own your emotions. There is nothing wrong with sympathizing and offering emotional support, but then it is time to step back and allow the person to deal with their emotions and learn their lessons—in their way—in their time frame.

If I'm Crazy, I Am In Good Company

Chapter 8

Energy Healing

To be very clear, no one has the ability to 'heal' you. For all health issues please seek professional advice.

For those that question whether anyone without a medical degree should offer advice on health or personal issues, I think Tracy Lee Nash's answer says it best. "Do you have a friend? Do you offer them advice? Well, should you if you don't have a degree?"

Today, there are multiple reasons more people are turning to non-traditional methods for healing everything from acne to terminal illnesses.

Energy healing is the manipulation of energy to restore the mental and physical health of one's body. Healing energy is also used for emotional grounding, an essential part of mental balance and clarity. This energy offers the receiver assistance that can help them cure or greatly relieve the symptoms of an illness, injury or emotional issue.

No matter what name a teacher or healer decides to use for channeling healing energy, all non-invasive procedures, with little or no physical contact, have similar components. During the sessions, healing energy is transmitted to the receiver through hands-on-healing, mental imagery, or both. If the healer is touching the receiver with their hands, the receiver will probably feel warmth or heat.

With mental imagery the healer, the receiver or both, use mental imagery to remove the illness. For an abnormal growth or rash, the visualization may show it shrinking until it disappears, or shattering into harmless matter. A young boy with a non-cancerous growth on his neck imagined Pac Man eating the cells and spitting them out. A woman with gallstones imagined hitting them with a laser gun and watching them explode into harmless dust partials. A man with chronic sinus infections imagined a hand scooping out the infection and swabbing the sinus lining with a disinfectant.

Mental imagery can be done at home or with the help of a healer. The point is to imagine the illness gone and the body healthy and whole. When receiving the energy people have said they felt a tingling sensation, warmth, and even a pulling sensation during the treatment. If the healer is empathic, they may experience the same sensations.

Recorded reports about gravely ill people, whose grave health issues were mysteriously cured, go back several centuries. I have heard stories about doctors who claimed test results were faulty when a disease disappeared. I have also heard of doctors taking credit for spontaneous healing. The claim was that a delayed reaction to drugs they pumped into the person's system cured the patient. Test results can be faulty and tests results can be accidently switched with another patient. It is also possible for drugs to be slow reacting. Still, neither claim honestly addresses terminally ill patients who have been sent home to die regaining their health.

Spontaneous recoveries have been attributed to God, Goddess, Shamans, medicine men, pagan chants, witchcraft and group prayers, to name a few. The methods and beliefs differ, but what these healers have in common is the ability to channel healing energy.

A Shaman's dance, a healer's herb teas, and magical chants and spells hold an aura of ritualistic mystery, cultural traditions and spiritual beliefs. At the core of the rituals is a faith in a divine power to channel healing energy to an emotionally or physically ill individual.

If you break a limb, a doctor will set the bone and immobilize the area with a cast or splints. If ill or injured, medication or surgery may be necessary. These steps facilitate healing, but they do not heal—the only person who can heal you—is you.

Not even in a Hollywood drama would a doctor say, 'I have done all that is possible, now let's explore alternative medicines and pray for a miracle.' Yet, 'go home and die in familiar surroundings, at best you have six months to live enjoy what's left, there is no cure,' and similar fatalistic comments, have been spoken by multitudes of physicians.

A friend made a comment that is as appropriate today as when her daughter was diagnosed with an inoperable brain tumor. If doctors were really concerned with a person's life, instead of delivering death sentence diagnoses, they would be the first to mention alternative healing methods that may offer a cure. Instead, doctors and insurance providers play God. They also make the patient and family members feel like criminals and Devil worshipers if they refuse a fatalistic diagnosis and seek help from intuitive healing practices that rely on faith and the ability to use universal healing energy, instead of drugs and at times, limited medical knowledge and procedures.

Healing Practitioners

The list of different techniques for healing could fill pages. The ones listed below, are the most widely known.

Applied kinesiology—also known as muscle testing. The theory is that every organ dysfunction is accompanied by a weakness in a specific corresponding muscle. The test is used to determine allergies, illness, dietary counseling, and the bodies need for herbal/nutritional supplements.

Acupuncture—Acupuncture is based on the theory that restricted energy flow (Qi) causes health issues. Thin needles are used to stimulate acupuncture points. The stimulation corrects the imbalanced flow of energy through meridians that are connected to the body's organs.

Crystal Healing—Using crystals and other stones to align chakras can be traced back to the Chinese and the American Hopi Indians. Each type of stone vibrates at its own level of energy, and holds its own healing power. When using stones for healing and chakra alignment, the receiver may feel a vibration. That vibration is said to be the healing energy resonating with the energy of the receiver.

Deep Tissue Therapy—also called deep tissue massage. This deep massage is a manipulation of the shallow and deeper layers of muscle and connective tissues. Besides general relaxation, deep tissue therapy realigns deeper muscles and tissues to help aid in the healing process.

Faith Healing—also called divine intervention. Practitioners of Faith healing believe that their religious beliefs, the use of prayer, and at times religious rituals, employ divine presence to use their power to initiate healing.

Psychic healing—the generic name for any type of healing energy where a healer channels healing energy and transfers that energy to a person by laying-on-of-hands, imagery or remote imaging. The energy can be directed to a specific chakra or area of the body injured or holding illness.

Reiki—Reiki means Universal Life Energy. Through a transferring of life energy, Reiki teaches that healing energy balances the spirit, mind, and body to their natural state of perfection. It is also believed that Reiki enhances spiritual growth and is beneficial to everyone—not just those that are ill.

Reflexology—Reflexology is a belief that energy circulates between human organs. When energy is blocked, it shuts off the flow needed for mental and physical health. Each organ is represented at different areas of the feet, hands and ears. It is believed that massage or pressure stimulation of the particular points will promote healing in the corresponding body part.

Spiritual Healing—without getting into an age old argument about spiritual versus Christian, spiritual healing uses prayer, meditation and faith in a divine power to facilitate personal healing.

At the core of all intuitive healing techniques is the belief that when the body's flow of energy is blocked, illness can manifest. To facilitate the healing process energy needs to freely flow through the body. This process includes the outer aura, the seven major chakras, the deeper layers of chakras through the body, and the meridians that are the acupuncture points.

Much like stress points, emotions can be held any place in the body and cause energy to flow slowly or block energy interiorly. For example, a person who has been told to control their emotions, or not talk about personal matters may have a block at the throat—the fifth chakra. A person who has been emotionally hurt may hold the emotions attached to that experience in the chest—the fourth chakra.

If you stood at a window and allowed a sunbeam to touch your hand, heat would caress your skin, and within minutes the heat would spread through your body. That is free-flowing energy—no thought or actions required.

Taking that a step further, if you imagined a wall of ice between your wrist and hand, you may be able to contain the sun's heat to your hand. That blockage would result in the hand feeling warmer (perhaps uncomfortably warmer), and the rest of your body feeling chilled. Now imagine melting the ice wall and allow the heat to once again flow freely. The hand cools as the heat flows freely through the body.

The same process happens when blocks in the body are removed; energy flows freely, the balance of energy is restored and the body has the power to heal itself.

Healers or facilitators of healing energy are not miracle workers. By sending healing energy to help the flow of the receiver's energy and increase the receiver's natural ability to heal, they assist a person. They can tell you what they see, sense or feel, but they should never diagnose disease and they cannot cure disease. If someone claims differently, offer them a wooden nickel for their time, and find a healer whose ego is not overshadowing reality.

No process is a comfortable 'one size fits all,' type of treatment. I have participated in cleansing rituals, and taken workshops, where containing laughter at what I perceived as gullibility and foolishness was a major effort. But my perception was counterbalanced by diehard believers with stories of spontaneous healing and shifts in attitudes that had been emotionally crippling.

Skepticism is healthy, a slight nervousness during a first session is natural, but if the process or the facilitator makes a person uneasy, or the person is asked to do anything unethical, they should end the appointment immediately. If a person wants money to remove a curse or claims to have a new wonder cure that a leprechaun bestowed upon them during the third full moon last July, they are a fraud.

It would be foolhardy to say that healing methods cannot be adjusted to suit a situation. Like me, many practitioners have studied many healing arts. With the ability to take the methods that work best for them, practitioners can offer unique experiences they developed by combining what they have learned, with what has worked well with clients.

Major health issues aside, the main reason a person seeks help from a healer is the everyday aches and pains, and emotional issues that affect daily life and the flow of healthy energy through the body.

Honesty Matters

The main question I hear from people who do not live close enough to work with me is how to locate an honest alternative practitioner.

Word of mouth is always the best recommendation, but that is not always available. Education is iffy because there are too many weekend wonder classes and internet classes offering instructions on tested healing technique and con-artist scams.

The basics skills for clearing energy or even hypnosis can be learned from books checked out from a library. However, books and instant certification classes cannot teach how to connect learned abilities with intuition and higher realm intuitive abilities. Also, without the use of intuitive powers, alternative healing practitioners offer their clients little more than a sugar coated placebo.

The truth is it may take several attempts to find an alternative health practitioner who is not a fraud or whose expertise is limited to what was taught in a weekend class or read in a book.

A person goes to a practitioner to find answers, emotionally and/or physically heal, and deal with the issue at a subconscious and conscious level. Even if their insurance company is paying the bill, the goal is to heal and step beyond the pain, not make the mortgage payments for someone's home for the next five years.

An ethical practitioner wants to help the client reach their goals and lose them as a client.

While not becoming a long-standing client is important, the time frame to reach a goal is dependent on many factors. The main one is the person's determination to change, heal and step beyond the past. A person who has never worked with intuitive energy, meditated, or done self awareness programs like yoga, should become comfortable with the program before expecting to see results.

Commitment is crucial! The well meaning shove given by a doctor, friends or family members does not count. With commitment, follow through to address the issues, and making changes, there should be a noticeable difference within a reasonable amount of time. Reasonable is determined by the situation, but if it feels like the process is not working, explore other alternative practices to find a process that works for you.

No matter what alternative healing program is chosen, at the end of a first session, a person will know if they are comfortable with the process and the facilitator. The process is a package deal. If a person likes the facilitator but not the process, or likes the process but the facilitator makes them uncomfortable, the process will not work.

A practitioner may use stones, aroma candles, essential oils or other tools to enhance a healing session. Notice the word enhanced—these items are not a cure and for most alternative medicine practices are not necessary. If the scent of lavender helps you relax, great. If taking a garlic supplement everyday stops people from crowding your personal space, wonderful. If rubbing a blue lapis stone makes you feel connected to universes wisdom, fantastic. The point is to remember that supplementary tools can enhance an experience, but for most healing practices they are not an essential part of the process.

A hundred odd years ago, traveling medicine men sold salves and bottles of tonic and restoratives. The bottles were filled with water, alcohol, and maybe a dose of opium. The con-artist's pitch claimed his products cured anything that ailed you. More likely it kept a person drugged or drunk, so they did not care.

Today's con-artist is more sophisticated, but the pitch is no different than the dollar bottle of swamp water and booze. Do not be persuaded by tales of a secret healing prayer given by a goddess who communicates with them every Friday the 13th. When pressed to buy leather pouches filled with feathers or herbs to ward off evil spirits, healing beads that are likely cheap glass, herbs that cannot be identified with certainty, or a hot pink rabbit's foot infused with special lucky powers, take a moment to ground in reality. Before spending money on trinkets, take a day to think about the purchase and the real reason the seller is peddling the items. If you are still drawn to purchasing stones, oils or any other item, visit a reputable shop that does not add false advertising or pressure to purchase immediately.

A reputable practitioner is concerned with helping their client; even if that means a flat rate session goes over the allotted time. Every practitioner deserves to be paid for their time, but being told that a session is over while raw emotions are exposed to the elements is an emotional landmine that an ethical practitioner will try to avoid.

Even if a practitioner uses their living room as a part-time office, they should act professional. If they are not willing to answer questions without demanding a payment or a paid consultation appointment, call someone else. That does not mean a person should take up an hour of their time because they are too lazy to do research, but before a first appointment reasonable questions should be offered without charge.

To put this all into perspective, I phoned a woman who was listed on a reputable website, to have a life-between-lives session.

We discussed her credentials as a counselor, hypnotherapist, and life-between-lives coach, which happened to be similar to mine. She talked like a space cadet, did not have an information form that could be emailed, and I had to repeat myself several times. I do these sessions regularly for clients. Looking forward to having a personal session, I ignored the warning signs and my gut feeling, and made the appointment.

Her office was a five hour drive away. The first appointment was for Friday. She said to be there no later than two, and to call to make sure her last appointment had left. Parked in front of the house that held several small offices, I left ten phone messages in an hour.

When she stepped out of the house, I stopped her. Oh, my, her phone was turned off—no apology. She said I should have knocked on her door. When I mentioned the sign that said she was in session, she said she never used that. When I asked why the sign was on the door, she shrugged—again, no apology. Now it was too late (her decision) for the preliminary interview.

The following morning, she arrived an hour late. After unlocking her office, she excused herself. Forty minutes later, she returned with a muffin and a latte. She could not find the tape recorder—she offered to drive to Wal-Mart to buy one. Then she remembered her boyfriend had her car. With an exaggerated sigh, she offered to take meticulous notes.

She had not read the questioner handed to her the previous day, so she asked questions and checked her watch twice.

She ate and slurped through her breakfast while hypnotizing me. At one point, she stopped the session so she could go to the bathroom.

These sessions usually run four to five hours, and she charged her hourly counseling rate multiplied by five. Barely two hours after the session started, the woman said the session would end in fifteen minutes. If there was someplace I wanted to visit 'quickly', to let her know.

As if I had been slapped, my eyes popped open—end of session. Her notes were two pages of chicken scratches. She promised to type them up and mail them. When I asked how much I owed her, she stated the full price for a five hour session. Didn't happen! Seriously, my thought was she should have paid me for putting up with her antics. Six weeks and two phone calls later, she mailed a photocopy of her notes.

If anyone else told me this story I would think they were embellishing the facts, but it did happen and has become a measuring stick for worst therapist awards. Still, nothing happens by chance, and every experience teaches a lesson. Space cadet, not returning calls, phone turned off, no respect, and lack of professionalism, were all powerful signs to cancel the appointment. I did listen to the warnings, but because I knew the process I did not think her scattered energy would interfere with my session. I was wrong! That experience taught me that credentials mean nothing if the practitioner has no common sense, no concern for the client, and no business ethics.

Each time someone tells me that an alternative healing practice does not work I ask why they made the appointment and how many times they went to the therapist. Enviably the answer is weight, smoking or stress, and they went to the practitioner once. One hypnosis session at war with twenty years of eating Twinkies; is it any wonder the Twinkies won?

One failed meditation session to find inner peace, compared to a lifetime of believing everyone else's needs come first. One hour of acupuncture to clear meridians and stop twenty years of nicotine addiction. The expectations are unrealistic, and guaranteed to produce failure. At the same time, a practitioner should be willing to discuss a time-frame, or the number of sessions they consider reasonable for a client to see or feel results.

Expectations are inevitable, but they need to be realistic. An intuitive healer can guide and make suggestions, but they cannot do the work for a client. It is like a diabetic choosing to eat a candy bar instead of an apple; success depends on making proper choices.

With any alternative medical practice, faith and trust in the process, and follow through, are the main ingredients to success. I prefer hypnotherapy to get to the core issue of a problem. From there I teach clients how to use healing energy. Once learned, it is a combination of techniques that can be done without the aid of a facilitator. The reason for learning to use alternative healing methods is simple, even when working with a healer, discovery is a personal journey.

Repetition will force a good editor to grab for the red marking pen. In a novel, repetition is tiresome and makes me skip paragraphs and pages. At the risk of offending everyone who gets it, I will say this one more time; the only person who can heal your body or your spirit is you. Physicians, healers, medication and herbal remedies facilitate the healing process, but they cannot mend a broken bone, cure an illness or heal a broken spirit.

There is a saying that time heals everything. For a broken bone, time to heal would be true, but time will not cure an achy bone when it rains or the jolt of pain when the bone is twisted a certain way.

Nor does time heal emotional trauma, erase the memories of physical pain, or erase the loss of a loved one. What happened is in the soul's memory bank and affects actions, reactions, and personalities. Experiences and the memories also formulate opinions based on personal truths. Like the monster under the bed, the memories lurk in the dark recesses of nightmares waiting to pounce. Post traumatic syndrome is a good example of hidden memories affecting every facet of one's life.

Whether working with a facilitator or working alone, manipulating healing energy to balance energy flow and promote healing takes patience, faith in the process, and a willingness to work to achieve success.

Nand Harjani is a businessman and teacher with offices in California, Hong Kong, India and Malaysia. Using intuitive insight, energy balancing and energy adjustments, he works with individuals and corporations. Raised in countries where intuitive powers are an accepted part of life, he has a deep understanding and respect for the powers within each of us.

In Nand's words, this is his story.

"The real question is not when I found out that I had several gifts, but when I found out that other people did use their abilities. There was my normal, but it was not everybody else's normal.

"I was seven or eight years old when the world began to revolve literally and figuratively with my being able to use those traits, we call them gifts; sometimes I call them burdens.

"I grew up in Asia where a lot of what we do today, what is labeled "psychic", was very much accepted then, and accepted to this day.

"It was very commonplace for folks (in Asia) to say that they are going to their astrologer or oracle to figure this or that out. Or to hear someone say, 'Uncle Joe just passed away so how can we help him on his journey to the other realm, and communicate with him?'

"My exposure during my younger and formative years was an interesting time because most folks did not consciously realize that they practiced a certain ritual, or a certain dogma that accepted the gifts I had. Yet, there was an unspoken 'understanding' that folks had which suggested that they could engage with people with my gifts for their needs.

"I was born in India but grew up in China. During this period, I was exposed to several cultures, spoke four languages fluently, and was surrounded by people who accepted gifted people like me with a high conscious level of healing and communication.

"It was in my eleventh or twelfth year of life that my gifts became prevalent in day-to-day life activities. As an example, in high school, I played rugby and could predict where the ball was going to land after a kick. The other players would go to left field, and I would go to right field and gain advantage for my team. I can still hear my coach yelling at me to be on the 'correct side of the field.'

"I moved to America to attend college. This was a cultural shock because the people I met and went to school with had no concept of how the Eastern world lived...so I kept things to myself.

"With time, my gifts progressed. I was able to see the potential of fellow classmates. I knew what an instructor wanted on a test, which actually made studying for the test more difficult. Intuitively, I knew how far I could push someone, and how to negotiate with people to achieve what I wanted. It was a dynamic time where I primarily used my gift for myself.

"Some of these gifts included the ability to see auras, and to see them in color, and a sense of feeling (ability to sense them). This gave me a clear and true understanding of the people with whom I interacted. Another gift is the freedom to travel to the different planes of existence (as an example a past life or the realm where Souls go when the body dies).

"I began to use my gifts to help others when I went to work in the corporate world. Intuitively, as an example, I knew if a new gadget/widget would be successful. People did not always believe me, but when they were willing to ignore negative forecasts, the gadget/widget would make it to market. I also understood what a person could and could not do, and had a clear understanding of how to help them connect with the path that would help them accomplish their destiny.

"When I left the corporate world, I started my business and have not looked back since.

"A number of years ago, a gentleman in Northern Europe contacted a student of mine, in Asia. I learned from my student that his significant other, a female in her late forties, had been diagnosed with cancer and was at that point in time almost at the fourth stage.

"This gentleman (he was both a gentleman and a gentle man) informed my student that his significant other's condition, according to her doctors, was very severe, and she was in much physical pain from the cancer. There was not much else they could do for her. My student suggested contacting me to see if anything more could be done.

"When the sick woman's boyfriend and I connected, I came to understand that the tumors that started in her lower body were growing throughout her body, and were now at her lungs.

"My first question was did the woman believe in the type of work that I do? The answer was "no". She was very religious, and believed anything outside the accepted medical profession was to be ignored. But he believed in energy healing and hoped that she would have an open mind. He added that his beliefs came from personal life experiences, and he wanted to give her every opportunity to live.

"I do not take my work lightly. I felt that there were a number of issues and concerns I as a healer, had to overcome first before accepting this assignment. These concerns and challenges included, did this woman really want to heal, or was it that her significant other wanted her healed? Was this case past a point of healing seeing that it was almost at the fourth stage? There were other concerns, but the two preceding ones were my main concerns. With these concerns in mind, I informed them I needed to meditate on this matter to understand if I was the correct healer for her needs and would get back in touch by the next day.

"By the following day, the conclusion was to move forward as I had the woman's permission via her "Higher Self." I also knew it would likely take about four or five separate one-hour sessions.

"These sessions would include: stopping the pain, stopping the spread of the tumors, shrinking the tumors, making sure that her own bodily defenses would 'kick in' and to provide assistance and support for this aspect of the healing process, and follow up to make sure all the work was done completely and permanently.

"Further, and to insure that we had quick results, I asked my student in Asia to help with a component of the process so that I could focus on my protocols. Thus began the process.

"The first session was conducted on the telephone. Basically, in addition to the cancer, her entire body was in much physical pain. This first session was the critical session because if the pain could not be stopped, then I could not proceed with the remaining components.

"I started the first session with a question to the woman; "Would you like me to help fix you?" To which, she replied, "Yes". This is what her higher self had said would happen and here it was. As I began, I could sense the fear in her. I also sensed the past life connections to her illness. I believe that we do not just heal the body in this realm but in many realms.

"As I was feeling the fear, I informed her that she and/or her significant other could ask as many questions of me as to what I was doing. I further explained that these were her sessions and I am of the mindset that folks need to know what is going on in regards to my work. This attitude helped ease her fear.

"As we began, she asked what she needed to do. I explained that I would ask her to do certain things, which would provide me with feedback on the work I would be doing to her body. For the next forty odd minutes, we went through her chakra systems.

"During this session, I worked on her chakras, both major and minor. These forty minutes were very intense in terms of the energy flow going through her body.

"My protocol requires me to simultaneously monitor the physical as well as the ethereal bodies and based on feedback I modify the energy flow to suit the work.

"The Chakra work, I find, has to do with healing across many lifetimes. In my protocol, this is done to make sure that I get to the point of inception of the problem that caused (in this life time) the illness. Simultaneously, during this time, there is focused energy work addressing the pain in the body.

"For the remaining twenty minutes, I concentrated and focused the healing energy towards the remaining pain in the body.

"Periodically, during this hour, I asked questions for verbal feedback on how she was feeling. Typically, during this time there might be a temperature change that a person can feel. Another thing I look for is vibrational sensation's that go throughout the body. That tells me how much energy her body can tolerate.

"During the last twenty minutes, her pain began to dissipate. To her surprise, by the end of the hour there was almost no pain in her body. That success made her eager to go forward.

"I explained to her that her body needed to become accustomed to my energy, and we needed to move slowly. I also explained that if the pain were held down for a twenty-four hour period we would reengage and proceed to the next step.

"The following evening we used Skype, so we had visual contact. With confirmation that the pain had not returned, we began the second session.

"With the ability to see her, I was able feel her lungs, feel her body and sense her feelings more directly.

"My goal for the session was to contain the tumors to one section of her body. About fifty-five minutes into the session I sensed we had achieved our goal. I believed that the work I had done would impact the tumors, begin to stunt the growth and possibly begin to shrink the tumors.

"Although the doctors had given up on curing the cancer, they were still monitoring the growth of the tumors. Her next appointment for the physicians to measure the size of her tumors using an ultrasound device was one week later. All of us felt we should wait a bit before moving forward with a third session.

"The day her doctor's appointment we connected through Skype. I could tell immediately that her energy level had increased, and her coloring had improved. She told me it was a miracle, not only had the tumors not spread, they were contained back to their original area in the lower body, and they had shrunk. This was confirmed by the ultrasound examination.

"She told me that with the pictures the doctors could measure the tumors. She said that the tumors had shrunk enough that there was a measurable difference in their size from the measurements taken previously. The physicians could not understand why, but not surprisingly, they did not give her a reason, and they did not ask if she had done anything different.

"In the third session, my intent was to shrink the remaining tumors. As I worked on her, I asked a lot of questions that to her were simple yes, and no answers, but they gave me guidance on where to direct the healing energy. I also made sure that her chakras; all the way down to the minor ones were clean.

"Three weeks after the third session, was her next doctor's appointment. The next evening and after her medical appointment, we met on Skype for our fourth session. During this session, she told me that the tests showed no tumors. Thinking the machine was malfunctioning the doctors moved her to a different machine and redid the tests—still no tumors.

"From our first phone conversation, where I sensed death within her, to her fourth session, her life force had come back. During this fourth session, I once again, went through her physical and ethereal bodies making sure that the cancer was 'gone' and that there were no further energetic connections to bring the cancer back. If there were any Energetic connections to her ethereal body, then that would have meant the healing had not been complete, and then the cancer would therefore, return.

"This was a very humbling experience for me. We kept in touch for about a two year period with no sign of cancer within her."

Chapter 9

Intuitive / Intuition

Intuition is accepting information without questioning or being consciously aware of the source. Together, intuition and intuitive awareness are the cornerstones of all intuitive power.

Without the willingness to recognize and accept information that is received in an illogical manner, meaning the information has not been read, taught, or overheard, intuition is nothing more than an easily ignored footnote.

Discussing intuitive visions and the voice within are not readily accepted, but admitting that intuition played a major role in making a decision is acceptable.

"I've built a multibillion-dollar empire by using my intuition." Donald Trump, entrepreneur.

"The intuitive mind tells the logical mind where to look next." Jonas Salk, medical researcher and inventor of the polio vaccine.

"The intuitive mind is a sacred gift and the rational mind is a faithful servant. We have created a society that honors the servant and has forgotten the gift. We will not solve the problems of the world from the same level of thinking we were at when we created them. More than anything else, this new century demands new thinking: We must change our materially based analyses of the world around us to include broader, more multidimensional perspectives." Albert Einstein, German theoretical physicist who developed the general theory of relativity.

"The only real valuable thing is intuition." Albert Einstein.

"Trust your hunches. They're usually based on facts filed away just below the conscious level." Joyce Brothers, American psychologist, television personality and columnist.

"I feel there are two people inside me—me and my intuition. If I go against her, she'll screw me every time, and if I follow her, we get along quite nicely." Kim Bassinger, American Actress

"Often you have to rely on intuition." Bill Gates, entrepreneur and founder of Microsoft Company

"Intuition comes very close to clairvoyance; it appears to be the extrasensory perception of reality." Alexis Carrel, French surgeon and Biologist who was awarded the Nobel Prize in Physiology of Medicine in 1912.

There are many more quotes that refer to intuition, but the point made by these well-known individuals is that they acknowledge their intuitive powers and trust the information to guide them professionally towards a successful outcome. The willingness to publicly state that intuitive information guided their success depicts an inner peace and acceptance that not all things can be logically explained.

To me, the word that exemplifies intuitive thinking is unconventional; going against the normal, what others expect or tell you to do.

Professionally and personally, I have collected a fair share of 'what were you thinking' moments. So I will share, a why didn't I listen lesson, with what worked.

I interviewed for a job that was a perfect fit, but my gut said the office manager (who would not be my boss) was trouble. When the office manager called and said, "I was told to call. You are the most qualified, so I'm sorry to say the job is yours." Seriously, those were her exact words. I should have listened to the 'voice within' when he stated that she held more power than the regional sales director and said no thanks. Instead, I endured eighteen months working alongside an insecure woman, and several discussions with the regional director who could not change the situation.

At another job interview, the company owner played the 'I am trustworthy because I am a born again Christian' theme. I wondered what dirty laundry he was hiding behind the pretense, but intuitively was being told to take the job.

It took three paychecks to figure out the owner's dirty secret—he and his wife were prolific liars, and they doctored shipping and return reports so they did not have to pay the sales representatives the commission they earned.

My love-hate relationship with computers is long standing, and well documented. Computer number one died a quick death one week after the warrantee ended. The gibberish on the backup disks could only be read by the Tar Babies on Mars. I mention this because my only résumé was on that computer.

When a sales position in the classified section of the paper caught my eye, I was on a tight schedule. With ten minutes to produce and fax a résumé, the half page of basic facts followed by 'call if you want more information,' would have won a blue ribbon in a worst résumé contest. There was no cover letter. My gut feeling was to send the resume anyway. The 'voice within' was laughing.

Two weeks later, I was asked to be at an interview the following day at half past four.

I was early—he was running late. Frankly, concerns about the interview were secondary. My main concern was not being late to teach a six o'clock adult education class on past life regression.

His first question was, "Why did you apply for the job."

'Insanity,' the inner voice quipped. Ignoring every interview rule, I went with the gut instinct and stated the truth. "Curiosity," I said. Before he could reply I added, 'I want to know what the company is going to do to clean up the problems. If the problems cannot be resolved, I do not want the job.'

He asked me what problems. After listing a handful, and what I thought needed to be done, I was hired.

Here is the intuitive message and the lessons learned. With the first job, logic overrode intuitive messages, and I spent eighteen months in purgatory paying for the error in judgment.

The second time, I listened to intuition and received a crash course training as a sale representative. More importantly, the company wholesaled a line of plush toys, and I won a national contest they held. By following intuition, the training, and the plush toy knowledge needed for the position I was being guided to, was provided.

Intuitively, I was pushed to ignore the Interview Bible of acceptable answers. The reward was a job that was fun and exasperating, and eventually led me to the next path of my journey.

Instant Messaging – Intuitively

A woman gets a feeling to call a friend she has not talked to in months. When she makes the call the person says, 'I was just going to call you.'

A man on a ski vacation breaks his arm. His friends are sympathetic, but no one wants to miss skiing on the fresh powder snow that is still falling. At the hospital waiting for x-rays, the man feels sorry for himself. As his mind wanders, he remembers how his mother made hot chocolate with extra marshmallows and whip-cream, when he was sick. His cellphone rings. When he answers, his mother says, 'What's wrong.'

A man is driving to work and traffic is flowing nicely. As he approaches a side street, he follows a sudden urge to turn onto the side road. He has only driven a block when he sees a good friend and co-worker. The hood of their car is up, and a puddle of rusty water is pooled around their feet. When he stops they say, 'I just tried to call you, but my cellphone is dead.'

On the way home, a woman stops at the grocery store. She passes the milk without a glance because she knows there is still half a gallon at home. But before leaving the store she backtracks, and adds a jug of milk to the cart. When she arrives home, she finds the milk cartoon on the kitchen table, tipped on its side. Trouble, a cat living up to his name, had a nice snack before leaving milky paw prints on the floor.

These are not random acts or reactions; thousands of similar stories happen every day. The person did not receive an audio command, or telepathic communication. The sudden feeling is a knowingness that defies any logical explanation, but provides an answer or causes a reaction.

Christmas Eve of 1980, I was enjoying the excitement of the last minute shoppers at a mall. A feeling, that I can only describe as a sober knowing washed over me. A familiar black-and-white picture of my grandmother smiling flashed before my eyes. A glance at my watch showed it was shortly after two.

I waited until five to call my folks. At that time, there was no caller ID, but without a hello, my mother said I could have waited until they had taken off their coats before calling. As I knew at an intuitive level, and my mother confirmed, my grandmother passed away shortly after two that afternoon.

Other than random telepathic connections with me and a family friend, my mother denies that she has any intuitive powers. Years later, I asked how she knew it was me on the phone and that I knew about Grandma's passing. She shrugged, and said that while making a list of whom to call, she just knew I had already received the message.

It is easy to brush aside insights as a good hunch, a freak accident, or even a random coincidence, but learning to trust instincts and paying attention to sudden hunches, can make life easier.

Intuitive Insight

I was in Los Angeles visiting my husband's great aunt. While discussing the past, my husband said he regretted not pushing past his step-mothers arguments to keep in touch with a much younger half sister. I told him that if he was serious to show me the family home.

The street, with well tended lawns and beautiful older homes, was quiet. Parked across the street from the house, I studied the neighborhood. I cannot say what I was expecting, if anything. While at Aunt Margie's house, the feeling that I could find *Kathy was a matter-of-fact knowing that it could happen. Parked across the street from the family home the feeling was stronger, but the how was a mystery.

Less than five minutes after parking, the front door of the home opened and a woman headed for our car. Time had not been kind to the woman, and she wore her bitterness like armor.

My husband muttered something rude, so there was no need to ask if she was the evil step-mommy.

Wanting answers, I took the, be nice route. Stepping out of the car, I introduced myself, offered my hand, and said it was nice to meet her. Ignoring me, she gave a throaty growl, narrowed her eyes, and demanded that we leave, or she would call the police.

When that failed to get the desired results, she asked what we wanted. She claimed Kathy was married and lived in another state. She refused to say where or give a last name. Then she shifted her stance, and said that if we left a contact number she would pass the information on to Kathy.

When we left I told my husband to take a left at the stop sign. Several miles and several turns later, we were in a neighborhood of houses built on two acre plots of land. Most of the houses had horses grazing in the fields behind the houses.

Spotting an equestrian center, I stated that Kathy worked there. My husband's expression clearly said he thought I was crazy.

In the office, I asked if Kathy was working, and if so, where could she be located. The woman did not deny that a Kathy worked there, but said she was the owner and would be happy to help me. Kathy's half-sister was dead, and she had been told that memories of a brother were a childhood fantasy. Saying that a brother was trying to locate Kathy, sounded like a lie. The woman's friendly demeanor vanished, and I was told to leave.

Leaving the stables, I directed us down several streets lined with houses. Three-quarters of the way down a street, I had him pullover. I had no vision, and the 'voice within' had been silent since leaving Aunt Margie's house. Working strictly on intuition, I cannot find the words to accurately describe the feeling of knowing we were at the right place.

No one was home, but a neighbor asked if he could help. When asked if he knew when Kathy would be back he could not answer, but he did not say, 'who is Kathy.'

After eating lunch, we returned to the house and the 'voice within' decided it was time to help. The number five whispered through me head. Five minutes or five o'clock, if the latter it would be a long wait. Five minutes later, a pickup truck, pulling a horse trailer, pulled into the driveway. Any doubts of the woman being the half-sister vanished when the she hopped out of the cab.

Writing this brings up the memories as if it happened yesterday. Being guided to the house and the equestrian center was surreal; a 'knowing' that disregarded logic, but felt so right it was as if I had been to Kathy's house before.

It is possible, that the genetic connection between the siblings created a bond that intuitively fed me information, or a forgotten lucid dream had shown me what would happen. It is also possible that the stars were aligned into a neon arrow that said, 'follow me.' Truth is, how it happened is not important. What matters is that it did happen, and two people connected at a time that would make a difference in their lives.

Elena Skyhawk has a powerhouse of stories that begin in early childhood. With intuitive abilities and questions that needed answers, her studies led her to become a Doctor of Medical Science. She is also a Reiki master, a Shaman.

In her words, this is her story.

"For me, knowing that I was different came very early. From an early age, I talked to animals, and they would listen and talk to me. At first I spoke out loud to the animals, but this too did not sit well with my mother.

"Then I realized that when the animals spoke I heard their voices in my head, not through my ears. So I began to talk to them quietly. At the time, I was too young to know the word telepathic.

"Much to my adoptive mother's dismay, after these encounters many of the animals would follow me home. After being scolded and told not to communicate with animals, I started projecting pictures to communicate with them. I do not know how I knew to do that, but being young and innocent I shared what I was doing. Again, I was warned not to talk to animals, but was never told why this behavior was inappropriate.

"Not communicating with the animals was impossible. Despite being told repeatedly that animals could not communicate with humans, I continued to hear their thoughts. And yes, they used to call me Dr. Doolittle.

"When I was five, I started having a very vivid dream. Our family would be camping, and a bear would appear and chase my family. After the bear attacked everyone in my family, the bear would approach me. The bear looked at me, but not in a threatening way. Still, I was scared and shaking. You can imagine the screams that woke everyone up. In a no nonsense manner, my mother would tell me that it was just a nightmare and to go back to sleep.

"When I was seven, the dream changed. The family would be hiking in the mountains, and a mountain lion would appear. The mountain lion would chase down my two brother's and parents', and I would be left all alone. Like the bear, the mountain lion would simply look at me, and I would wake up screaming.

"When I was six, we visited Yellowstone Park. At one of the scenic lookouts, a black bear charged up over the mountain. When the bear reached the parking area, she started to chase my family.

"My dad, followed by my mom, ran towards the car. My older brother was ahead of me. My Grandma, holding onto my little brother for dear life, was mere steps behind me. When I reached the car, my parents' and older brother were safely inside with the doors closed. I opened a door, and my Grandma slid inside with younger brother, and I followed.

"As soon as the door was closed, the bear reached the car. With her head at window height, the bear looked directly at me. Clearly I heard her ask, 'Are you okay?' Scared to death, I could not help but think that my dream had become reality.

"At twenty-eight, I met my first spiritual teacher. She explained that the bear and the mountain lion were my power animals; here to make sure I survived the abuse I suffered at the hands of my adopted parents'. The animals could not do anything on a physical level, but on a spiritual level they made sure our connection stayed clear and strong.

"A friend and I visit Indian ruins on New Year's Day to meditate, and think about the year ahead of us. One of the rooms is a circle, which for Native American's is very sacred. During a meditation, Spirit came in and told me to 'flow like the water.' I'm very intuitive, but this made no sense to me.

"I admit I can be a bit hard-headed and a little dense at times, but not knowing the meaning behind the riddle drove me crazy. I talked it over with my mentor, a shaman and teacher, and he told me that with patience the answer would come.

Instead, I think I imagined every way water could flow, but it felt like the harder I concentrated, the more elusive the answer became.

"Three months later, I attended a shamanic class at the Salt River. Serge, the same teacher who told me to have patience, asked us to locate a stick and make a prayer stick.

"On the walk back to the river, after finding my stick, I was debating on whether to stay by the river and meditate, or go to my usual place up on the mountain.

"My back was to the stairs leading to the parking lot when a deep masculine voice, I did not recognize said, "Get over here!" I froze in my tracks. Too scared to turn around, my first instinct was to run or to yell for help, and hope the people putting boats in the river would hear come to my rescue.

"Before I could move the man said, "I said, Get over here!"

"I do not appreciate being ordered to do anything, but one thing struck me as odd. If the man was going to attack me, why was he ordering me to 'get over here?'

"Drawing every ounce of courage I possessed, I turned. There was no one there. More preciously, no human energy was behind me. What stood behind me was an ancient tree, lush with new growth and vibrating with energy. Split by lightning, one part of the tree trunk stood tall and grew towards the sky. The other half of the ancient tree had fallen. The exposed center of the trunk now formed a softly curved bench.

"Okay, I communicate with animals and understand that people find that difficult to believe, but was it possible for a tree to tree?

"Feeling a little foolish, I said aloud, "Are you talking to me?"

"You see anyone else around?" I heard the words telepathically. I would have sworn the first two commands were shouted verbally, but now I was not positive.

"Of course I'm talking to you, now get over here!" The tree's spirit needed lessons in manners, but instead of pointing that out, I approached the tree. Having gotten what he wanted, he told me to sit and rest on him. I set my backpack on the ground. Lying on his trunk, I closed my eyes.

"I lost track of time, but I heard a family descend the stairs, and a young boy commented on the fisherman sleeping on the tree. Funny as I did not have a fishing pole but then I remembered I was still holding the prayer stick.

"When all was quiet, I heard, "Let go of the pain, let Mother Earth receive it."

"I rested my hand on the ground and asked the earth to please help me release and all pain and emotions that were taking a toll on me. Finally, I heard, "Look at the river and tell me what you see."

"I see a Heron, a large rock, and people in boats going down the river." I replied and heard an exasperated sigh as if I was trying his patience.

"Look again, but this time look at the water. What do you see?"

"There's a large rock in the center of the river. When the water hits the rock, it splits around the rock and some water shoots up and over the rock.

"I swear the tree sighed.

"When Spirit told you to flow like the water this is what they meant. When obstacles get in your way find a way to get around them or go over them. Flow like the water!"

"I knew that, so why had it taken three months, and a talking tree to teach me a valuable lesson? As suddenly as I asked the question, I had the answer. I had allowed life to get in the way of my knowing; that part of me that intuitively knew what to do, even when the action looked like a one way road down a dead-end track."

Chapter 10

Medium

A medium or sensitive is a person who, through various means, communicates with spirits. A clairvoyant sees information from the past, present, and future. I stress this because they are different intuitive abilities; one power is not connected to the other. A clairvoyant may see and communicate with spirits, but according to several mediums I interviewed, being a medium does not necessarily take them down the yellow brick road to clairvoyance. In fact, one medium compared understanding what a spirit wants to communicate, to putting a giant jigsaw puzzle together.

The written history of oracles, shamans, sorcerers, mediums and witches (herbalist) having the ability to communicate with Spirits, dates back thousands of years. Depending on the beliefs of the culture or the individual, dances, chants, sacrificial offerings, gifts of food, prayer, magic spells, and plants that alter the perception and are believed to enhance the mediums abilities and clarity, have been used to enhance the medium's intuitive abilities.

It is believed that rituals were a sign of respect to God, Goddess, Spirit, Angels or other worldly beings who offered information. I believe rituals were also used as a window dressing to give the impression that intuitive abilities were sacred powers only available to a chosen few.

Rituals are still used today. Burning colored and scented candles is a common practice during healing sessions. Like tea leaves and a crystal ball, a candles flame can be used as a focal point; a type of self hypnosis that allows distractions to fade into the background while the medium or practitioner focuses their energy on the spirit body.

I have never seen a ghost wearing a white sheet and floating in the air. Nor have I ever heard a ghost act Halloween scary. That does not mean they do not exist, it just has not been my reality. I have seen and talked to Spirits who wanted information conveyed to clients. What they had in common with the comments from my 'voice within' is personalities and attitude.

Most people do not want to encounter anything that goes bump in the night or think about ghosts watching their every move. However, you can, and probably do, communicate with

Spirits while asleep. During dreams the soul, the part of you that controls the subconscious mind, can experience direct communication with Spirits. The Spirit may also be part of a scene and convey messages through actions and comments during the dream.

During a recent restless night, a dream seemed to pick up where it stopped during moments of wakefulness. When I awakened, all I could remember of the dream were the last words said by my father, 'reliability matters.' I had not gone to bed thinking about any situation, but the words allowed closure with a situation that for several days had been weighing on my mind.

A friend had a dream about sitting on a horse on a merry-go-round; her parents' sat on either of her. As the music played, and the horses they sat on went up-and-down, the parents talked about her inability to see that life was a matter of balancing the highs and lows. She said it took a day to shake the feeling that the dream happened in 'real time'.

Similar to audio or clairaudience intuitive abilities, spirits also communicate through audio perception. The inflection of their voice will sound like the person when they were alive. Their personality may also come through. If they were serious, a tease or bossy when alive, using those familiar traits is a form of confirmation that they really are communicating with you. This communication should not be confused with negative audio replay that undermines thoughts, perceptions and emotions.

A client, in an abusive relationship, shared this experience. At a hospital emergency room, she was lying on a gurney waiting to be wheeled into x-ray. Her lip was split, one eye was swollen shut, and a shoulder was dislocated. She was silently crying when she heard a woman say, 'you don't need to put up with abuse.' She opened her good eye, and saw that she was alone in the waiting room. When she closed her eye, she heard the words again. This time she recognized the voice as her mothers. 'You did,' she thought and held her breath waiting for a reply. Her mother had always maintained that marriage was forever, no matter what. So her mother's comment that staying in an abusive relationship was wrong surprised her. While waiting for the doctor, the woman also heard her mother say she would help give her strength to leave. The woman thought about what her mother said and vowed to leave after she got her next paycheck. Then her mother said, 'Don't go home!' Because of the urgency of the words and memories of her mother's death from a fall down a flight of stairs she took the advice.

For some mediums, empathy and a 'knowing' or gut feeling work together to give a sense of presence when a Spirit is in a room. There may also be a sense of what the Spirit looks like in human form. 'I sense a woman, in her mid forties, with brown hair, or I sense a spirit guide, who walked this earth as a Shaman,' would be typical comments when a person is using empathy and intuitive sense.

If a guide appears while I am with a client, the air around the guide shimmers with energy, and there is a sense of whether the energy is male or female. Seldom do I receive communication from these Spirits. It is as if they are there only to give the client moral support.

I have seen and talked to Spirits who wanted information conveyed to clients. So far, none of them wore a white robe, had wings, a halo, or a golden harp. Instead, they wore outfits, that when described, were recognized by family and friends.

Seeing a Spirit is not something that can be easily ignored or forgotten. A misty vision, semi-transparent, and dense but without substance are accurate descriptions. Like us, Spirits are energy, so there is a good chance that their ability to generate energy determines how they appear.

Late one night, I had a dramatic encounter with a Spirit when a feminine voice told me to open my eyes. Since I had just settled into bed, and the room was pitch-black, I could not imagine why I needed to open my eyes, but curiosity was stronger than any sense of fear. At the ceiling, hovering over me, a face covered the entire ceiling. Her curly hair was jet black and her eyes were dark. The nose was narrow, her complexion pale. Startled, I simply said, 'hi.'

The Spirit, offered a slight smile and said, 'Please tell *Josh I am really sorry.' Thinking of the only Josh in my life I said, 'He won't listen, so why would I do that?'

'Not that Josh, *my* Josh,' the spirit snapped as if I should have known that. 'Please tell him if I could change the past I would. I am very sorry.'

Then she vanished. Half expecting her to reappear, I did not close my eyes for several minutes. During that time, I remembered a client's appointment for the following afternoon. After telling Josh the story, he confirmed that my description of the woman matched his mother, a woman who had been deceased for several years.

With the exception of one funeral, I have always felt the presence of the deceased. With three memorable exceptions, the energy is the shape of a body but there is not enough energy to generate features. The form shimmers as it stands by the casket, a family member, or floats above the room.

At my father's funeral, my husband and brother-in-law sat in the pew behind me. Several times during the funeral, I heard my father chuckling. His presence was strong, but there was no shadow or haze that indicated he was present. Standing to sing a hymn, I turned. My father stood between my husband and my brother-in-law. Semi-transparent, Dad was wearing his

Air Force tan dress uniform. His smile was wide, and he looked young and healthy. At the end of the twenty-one gun salute, I felt a feathery brush of air against my shoulder. When I glanced back, he was gone. Later, I asked why there had been a space, wide enough for someone to sit between the men. With a shrug my husband said, 'Don't know.'

A funeral for my husband's uncle was held at a large church. During the service, it was announced that Chuck's favorite songs were going to be played. At that moment, Chuck appeared. He stood with a shoulder leaning against a wall and one ankle was crossed over the other. His arms were crossed, the long sleeves of his shirt were rolled up, and he wore a cowboy hat. His spirit was so dense he looked alive, and I sensed that he was totally at peace. When the songs ended, he faded from view. When I described what I saw to his widow, she said the stance and the cowboy hat was typical of him when he had been younger.

At a memorial service, I asked directions to the restroom. Imagine my surprise when the directions led me to a small viewing room. Standing beside the open casket a woman watched me. It took a second to realize I was seeing Linda's spirit. She gave a soft chuckle and said, 'You weren't expecting me?' Her body was semi-transparent, but her facial features were so clear it was easy to forget she was a spirit. Orally, I admitted that I had expected to see her in the room where everyone was gathered. Thinking she had been cremated, I said it was the open casket that startled me. She smiled as if what I had said was funny. Before she could comment, two young boys entered the room and she turned her attention to them. A few minutes later, when the room was empty, I returned but Linda was gone.

When I asked my inner voice why seeing spirits is the most elusive of the intuitive senses he laughed, and reminded me of the 'oh damn' moment when I saw the open casket. Personally, the presence of a spirit is calming; an open casket is just plain creepy. But my reaction is atypical.

No matter how a person feels about seeing a spirit, I believe it is possible for everyone to use their intuitive senses to communicate with family and friends who have passed over. All it takes is an open mind, patience, trust and a desire to talk to the person.

Simone Browne lives in Australia. At a young age, she sensed her intuitive gifts, but like so many I have talked to, Simone had to go through life's trials before truly appreciating the significance and power of her intuitive gifts.

In her words, this is her story.

"From as young as I can remember, I would often know what someone was going to say before they spoke. Just before I

I R Plummer

intuitively received information I would feel sick in the stomach and feel the flutter of butterflies. I also knew when something different was going to happen, or I was going to get into trouble for something.

"Again, at a young age, I could sense, what I now know to be, spirits around me. I also had imaginary friends whom I talked to. I could not see the spirits, but could hear them and feel their presence with me. The spirits were mainly children's voices, but there was an older lady that talked to me quite often. I never felt the need to share this with my family as I had accepted that this was a normal thing and thought everyone else was the same. In my family, it became a bit of a joke as I talked in my sleep. I did not remember the dreams, but now know that during those dreams I was in fact, communicating with spirit.

"When I was eleven, my grandfather passed away. At his wake, I felt his presence very strongly, but I could not see him. For a long time after his death, I saw him in my dreams and often sensed him around me during the day. At the time, I dismissed the feelings as I was not fully in tune with what I was receiving intuitively.

"I was a sensitive child, and that did not change as I matured into my teens. I often, mentally and verbally when alone, talked to myself about whatever was going on at the time, and quite often I heard answers or someone talking to me. At one point, I thought I was going crazy and felt quite emotionally confused, but I did not tell anyone how I felt or talk to them about the inner voice that spoke to me.

"When I was eighteen, a girlfriend and I visited a psychic. I was surprised that the woman knew so much about me and frankly her predictions and accuracy frightened me. However, curiosity was also there, so I attended a few more 'readings' in the years to follow. Most of what the woman predicted for my friend and I happened. Around the same time I met Jenny, she was very spiritual and read tarot cards. I spent many hours at her home drinking coffee and discussing paranormal activity. Jenny taught me bits and pieces about how to read the cards, but I discovered that I picked up on things about Jenny without using the cards. At the time, I did not question how I knew the information, it was simply there.

"At age twenty-three, my other grandfather passed away. A few days before he passed over, I had a private visit with him at the hospital. I distinctively remember seeing a beam of white light around him. At his funeral, I felt his presence and above his coffin was the same white light that was in his hospital room. During the funeral, a warm calmness came over me and after that he appeared in my dreams. On one particular occasion, I woke up in the middle of the night to his voice calling me, "Mony", short for Simone. I could not see him, yet I smelled the aftershave that he used to wear.

"I became involved in a relationship with a man whose father died while he was young. On nights we spent at his family home, I heard footsteps in the hallway. Instinctively, I knew it was my partner's deceased father. One night, I awoke from a deep sleep with the feeling of someone pressing on my chest. I felt hands around my throat, and felt as if I was pinned to the bed and could not move. When I opened my eyes the feeling on my chest and neck stopped. Looking around, I saw my partner's father standing at the end of the bed. That was the first time I actually saw a spirit.

"During a holiday to Hawaii, spirit gave me information about a woman who sat alone at the horseshoe shaped bar where we had just ordered a drink. I told my partner that she had just split from a nasty relationship and she had just been through a litigation matter that had to do with her former employment.

"I left the bar for a few minutes, and when I returned my partner was talking to the woman. She confirmed that everything I had said was accurate. She lived in New York, and as we chatted she wanted to know more. By this stage, information was just flowing, and I relayed several pieces of information about her family. A couple of weeks after we returned to Australia she telephoned from New York and confirmed that the information I'd told her was accurate. She asked if I could do a phone 'reading' for her sister and a friend. I declined, because at that point, I did not have the confidence.

However, the experience made me think about the possibility of going down that path.

"After that experience, I started receiving more information from my guides about friends and complete strangers. Whenever I shared the information, the people would confirm that the information was accurate.

"One night, sitting on a porch, I 'read' for a girlfriend. I told her I felt very sore around the breast area and was being shown an image just as if it were real. It was in front of me as if I could touch a broach with a pearl in it. My friend went inside and returned with a little white box. Inside was the broach, exactly as I had described. It had been left to her by an aunt who had passed with breast cancer.

"After that evening, I decided to study psychic abilities and attended classes on clairvoyance, tarot and meditation. The classes taught me how to meditate properly, and although the tarot cards were interesting, I again discovered that I was able to read more accurately without them.

"After the birth of my first child, I stopped 'reading'. Then my father was diagnosed with brain cancer, my youngest child was diagnosed with autism and the relationship with my partner dissolved. It was a very emotionally testing time.

"Six months after my father's diagnosis he fell into a coma. At his bedside, I held his hand and spoke to him. I knew that he heard me because each time I spoke his breathing pattern changed. Whilst holding his hand, I felt warmth and a tingling feeling come over my body. As I had seen with my grandfather, a beam of white light appeared.

"While preparing to leave the house, I saw my young son at the door to my father's bedroom. I called to him, but his eyes were fixated on my Dad. I walked to the door and saw that the white light had become brighter and larger. My dad passed away early the following morning. That night, when I went to bed, I heard my Dad call out, "Simone, it's me, your poor old Dad." I told him that I could hear him, and he told me that he would not leave us. Since Dad's passing, I became fully aware of him around my children, and I speak to him regularly.

"My dad's presence and knowing my guides were there to help, gave me the confidence to start 'reading' for people again. Taking a friends advice, I agreed to do 'readings' for people on a phone line. Working for two popular psychic phone lines, I was thrown in at the deep end and off I went like a rocket!

"At times, skeptics called the psychic phone line and tested me; they were my favorite! I knew instantly when I was being tested and had great pleasure in providing them with a high level of accuracy in their 'readings'!

"One woman started off by asking me was I real, how was it possible to do a 'reading' for someone over the phone? I saw a great big packet of M&M's, and told her that spirit was telling me that she had been eating too many M&M's! I went on to tell her that she needed to change her son's mattress. It had a hole in it and he was not comfortable on it, hence his restless sleeping patterns, particularly over the past three weeks. This woman was completely blown away and from that moment on became a regular client.

"Another woman called and explained that she was very skeptical as past 'readings' had not been a very good experience. Instantly, spirit showed me a baby girl in her mother's arms being rocked, and I heard the mother singing, Rock a Bye baby. I started singing the song and told her what I was seeing. Her mother, who had passed over approximately five years before, sang that song to her as a baby and even as she grew older.

"The mother also showed me a gold bracelet that had been hers. She had left it to this woman when she passed over. I described the bracelet in detail including the etching on the back. The woman started crying as she could not believe how accurate I was. It was actually quite lovely as the mother then began to pass on messages through me. The mother talked about issues that were going on in the woman's life. That gave confirmation that the woman's mother was around her and was protecting her. This woman also became a regular client of mine.

"The majority of clients were people wanting advice and guidance on issues to do with love, relationships and career and finance. At times, working with callers was difficult because they did not want to accept what you told them. Hoping for a different answer, they would continue to call with the same questions. I came to the conclusion that there are some people that you cannot help entirely if they are not prepared to help themselves.

"Working the phone lines built my confidence. When I felt like I was being directed to stop working for the phone lines, I went out on my own, and have not looked back. It really is a great feeling knowing that I am able to use the gift that I have to help others when in need."

If I'm Crazy, I Am In Good Company

Chapter 11

Psychometrist / Psychometry

In 1842, Joseph Rodes Buchanan, a scientist, faculty dean and professor at the Eclectic Medical Institute, in Covington, Kentucky coined the term psychometry. The word means, soul measuring. Psychometry is a form of scrying which is using a crystal ball, mirror, tea leaves, a bowl filled with water, or other objects to receive visions or information.

All living beings, humans and animals, generate and transmit energy. Inanimate objects like, your iPod, Smartphone (really, you only think it is your best friend), car keys, jewelry, favorite CDs, the refrigerator; items you touch regularly, absorb energy. Think of your energy as a unique fingerprint that cannot be removed with a strong detergent or time.

Psychometry is the ability to hold or touch an object and receive information about the owner or the previous owners of the object. The information can be received through, sense, smell, audio and vision, or all four together.

Object Psychometry

This is the most commonly known form of psychometry. A person touches an object, and they have a vision, the 'voice within' offers insight, or they receive impressions of people who left their energy on the object.

Another form of object psychometry is used daily.

A person is car shopping, and spots the perfect car. They slide into the driver's seat, and enjoy the soft supple feel of the leather seats. The console looks like it belongs on a 747 jet—powerful and high tech. They turn the ignition key and the engine purrs to life. The car is perfect until the excitement settles down, and they take the car for a spin around the block. They cannot put a finger on the why, but they feel uneasy, and no longer feel comfortable in the car. Back at the showroom, they walk away without hesitation.

A woman finds a dress that is suitable for work or a nice dinner out with friends; her best friend agrees. Instead of heading to the cash register, she hesitates, and hangs the dress back on the rack.

The price on a sports coat has been reduced to half price. A man imagines the snazzy impression the new coat will project with his boss or girlfriend. The jacket fits like it was made for him, but while checking out the fit in the mirror he does not feel comfortable. The dream shatters as he walks away.

The car, dress, and sports coat are brand new, but they were produced, packaged, shipped and stocked by humans. That is a lot of handling, and a lot of energy infused on an item. For the majority of items the energy left by a few seconds or hours of handling is minimal, but negative energy is heavier and leaves a stronger imprint.

Anyone who does not believe that evil exists does not watch the news, read a newspaper or search the internet. People who commit horrific crimes, have families and friends, and lead normal lives where they may attend church, coach soccer games, and attend dance recitals. They also work; perhaps to assemble a red car, sew a pretty dress, or cut the material for a sports coat.

What was experienced when choosing to walk away from what appeared to be the perfect item was psychometry—a strong sense of someone's energy disturbing your energy. The item itself is not possessed, or evil, but it can transmit traces of negative vibrations left by others.

On an emotional level, the negative energy might not register with a friend, a spouse or a salesclerk, but what counts is how you felt. If the person had purchased the car, chances are they would never feel comfortable while driving. The dress or sports coat may get worn once or twice, but more likely, the clothing would get pushed to the back of the closet and forgotten.

To experiment with psychometry, ask friends who have family jewelry if you can try to pick up the energy imprinted on the item. Write down your impressions, so that a person's expression does not influence you. When done, read what you have and let them confirm or deny the accuracy.

If the object is small, the most common way to receive information about the object is to hold the item. With large items, running a hand over the item is a good way to pick up the energy.

Personally, the only thing I receive when touching an object is dusty fingers or static shock. However, I met an antique shop owner in Virginia who used psychometry to authenticate pieces he purchased at auctions and from estates. He said that when holding an old object, like a pocket watch that was handed down from father-to-son, impressions, scents and snapshot visions, would jump back-and-forth through the decades.

Touching an open salt that was on the counter, he said he saw flashes of formal dinners, candlelight and children sitting at a table. Since the salt cellar was made in the 1880's, I could have said the same thing and not been wrong.

No doubt my expression was not filled with awe, because he asked if he could hold the antique ring I wore. He had my full attention when he said I had received my dimples from a female relative who had lived in another country. He also saw matching rings, and a redheaded man wearing the second ring.

The ring is one of a matched set; custom made for my great-great grandparents who lived in Sweden. Family pictures confirm the dimples go back at least to my great grandmother. My uncle, a redhead, inherited the man's ring. The shop owner also mentioned pipe smoke, lavender perfume and the initial C. My grandmother's name was Claire. Her father and grandfather, the man who had the rings made, were named Carl.

A few years later, a hypnotherapy client mentioned that she could 'read' objects. She knew nothing about my abilities, but she had just spent time exploring previous lives, so my interest in intuitive abilities would be expected.

I enjoy talking to people who use their intuitive abilities. Unfortunately, too many people who claim to be 'psychic' are more interested in impressing people than using their abilities appropriately. There are exceptions, but using intuitive abilities is no different than a baby who learns to crawl, walk and then run. With baby steps, most people's powers increase as confidence is built, but when intuitive abilities are abused, the abuser can stall at the crawl or baby step stage and never progress further.

So, when the client commented on psychometry, I smiled and said 'really' or something else just as noncommittal. The smile was like a green light. She talked about 'reading' for friends and said since arriving she'd had difficulty ignoring the information being offered from the area rug beneath her feet. She proceeded to tell me that the rug was at least seventy-five years old and had been originally purchased in England. A swift vision of the outlet store where the rug was purchased made me smile. Without commenting, I made a mental note to rent a rug cleaner.

The furnishings in the office are sparse. Oak rockers, lamp tables, and a plant stand are antiques, origins unknown. I know the history of a woman's oak desk and a marble bust.

With my smile now a little strained, I asked if she could tell me anything about the desk or the bust. Did I feel guilty inquiring about items where I know the history? Absolutely not!

Running her hands over the desk, she frowned. According to her, the original owner lived on the east coast. An unhappy woman, she died at a young age after a long-term illness. The desk had changed hands several times, and because she saw cornfields she thought one of the owners was a farmer.

Here are the facts. The desk was made by the Larkin Co, in Buffalo, N.Y. and shipped to Goshen, Indiana—the Larkin Co instruction label and the shipping label are still on the back of the desk. The desk remained in the same house until the heirs sold the desk sometime in the 1970's. The buyer, lived in Goshen, and died in the eighty's after a long battle with cancer. He was in his fifties. His widow moved to Idaho and sold the desk to me.

Running her hands over the bust, she said the sculptor and the woman who posed for the bust were longtime lovers. She also saw the bust being crated, a ship and the bust being placed in a basement storage area where she said it remained for a long time.

Here are the facts. In 1875, my great-great grandmother traveled from Sweden to Italy with her ten year old son so he could learn marble sculpturing from a master. How long she stayed in Italy is unknown, but she was the model for the bust. The bust was shipped to America in 1894. I do not know when my grandmother inherited the bust, but for over forty years it was at the entrance to a hallway, in my grandmother's basement apartment in Chicago. A clear plastic cover over the bust and pedestal protected it from the grime that seeped through the sidewalk level windows.

Like any intuitive ability, a person can misinterpret images received through psychometry. I believe the woman received information about the pieces. Not knowing that I knew their history, she did what a lot of intuitive people do when the spotlight is on them; she embellished or put her own spin on what she saw to make the information more interesting.

Location Psychometry

The most common name for this experience is déjà vu. It is that feeling of knowing that overcomes a person when stepping into a place for the first time. If standing in an old homes foyer, the person knows that the kitchen is downstairs and to the left. The master bedroom has a bay window, built in walnut cabinets, and a door leading to a nursery. When the knowledge turns out to be accurate, there is no logical explanation.

While many people have experienced this form of psychometry at least once, it is common for people to laugh off the experience or brush it aside as nonsense or lucky guesses.

While attending hypnotherapy school, I hypnotized a woman whose husband was in the Air Force. During a tour of duty in Nevada, they spent weekends visiting ghost towns. Several experiences of walking into old rickety buildings and 'knowing' how it looked when people lived in the town, lead her to a local library to do research. Several books that documented ghost towns included pictures of the building where she experienced the déjà vu. The reality and what she felt while walking through the places were not exact, but close enough to make her question reincarnation.

If you do not believe in reincarnation, equate déjà vu to information being fed to you by former occupants of the public building, church, or house. I will not say ghosts because I do not believe the feeling has anything to do with a haunting. The energy that former occupants left is either still very strong, and/or your energy and the energy in the room vibrate at the same level.

Person Psychometry

There is a reason for terms like; the room was thick with tension, the room pulsed with anger, I felt the anger roll off him, and the room was warm and cheery.

Think about the times you walked into a room and felt the tension or the mood of the people inside before they spoke. Did you feel uncomfortable, nervous, or uncertain you should enter or speak? If you did they are common reactions, do not brush them aside as nonsense.

Thoughts are energy. That energy creates a field of energy that surrounds us and affects the people around us. It only takes one person with empathic powers to emotionally connect with people fed up with government, working conditions, or the quality of the French fries at the local drive-in to create a mob mentality of violence.

They call television evangelist and high profile politician's charismatic. But what makes an evangelists ability to touch emotions and draw in millions of dollars a year, different than the pastor or priest at the local church who does not flash a toll free number every five seconds requesting donations?

Why are people willing to vote for a smooth talking proven lair when there are qualified candidates running for office?

Let's go back to thoughts are energy. The thesaurus for charismatic includes the word magnetic, which is energy. Charismatic men and women know how to use empathic energy to charm people.

You walk into a room where loud, obnoxious Uncle Ben has set a somber mood as he makes certain everyone hears his latest tirade. You turn to leave, but he sees you. In a single breath his energy shifts as he grabs you in a bear hug, and teases you about your latest girlfriend or the purple hair that makes you look like a Troll doll. The people in the room relax, and until Uncle Ben starts the next rant, he is the life of the party.

That is person psychometry. Under the guise of charisma or charm, person psychometry is the ability to read people or a situation, and with the help of empathic energy control a room, a stadium, or a nation.

The belief that first impressions are important is not a myth. Besides judging a person by appearance, we automatically use psychometry to gage our comfort level. If a person's appearance is unkempt, but the person is sociable, conversation will flow easily. If the person's persona is offensive, elegant clothes will not counterbalance a negative first impression.

The same is true about surroundings. For example, if a formal dining room was once a battleground for political discussions during Sunday dinners, the memories will continue to affect the impression of the room and the ability to relax— even when the people who caused the arguments are not there.

Think about the last time you entered a room where you knew no one. After spotting the cute blonde or handsome hunk that is the center of attention, who caught your attention? Who were you drawn to? Appearance, body language, and facial expressions are key factors in the mini drama, but it is also a form of people psychometry at work. Energy meeting energy and feeling a compatibility that says, 'hello, I am a friend.'

Business functions are staged with lights and music, and filled with what very often sounds like canned laughter on

Prozac. The room is packed with people, and there is no need to touch anything to feel the dizzy array of emotions, that is people psychometry.

Some people thrive in this type of energy and may want to see what type of mischief they can stir up. Some individuals will find a quiet corner to people watch. Others will avoid the worst of the high maintenance energy as they work their way towards a person or group whose welcoming energy holds no menacing undertones.

Whatever your choice of action would be, understand and accept that your natural intuitive abilities will automatically read energy and help guide your choices.

Denise Lambie lives in Australia. She is a highly skilled internationally known medium, who motivates and inspires people globally through her ongoing work as a life coach, NLP practitioner, holistic massage therapist, and meditation facilitator. She trained under Doreen Virtue as an Angel Intuitive and as, a Reiki Master she teaches the healing art.

In her words, this is her story.

"I have been able to contact spirits since I was a little girl, but I kept this gift quiet to all but family and close friends for fear of ridicule.

"I have vivid memories of a past life, and remember as a child seeing green glowing figures of old men's faces at night when I lay in bed. I also saw a lady in white who I knew was my beautiful guide Celine.

"The visions scared me, so I would go running into my mum and dad's room, or I would hide under the bed covers. I have always been sensitive to my environment, but as a child my mum constantly told me to 'stop being so sensitive.' Because of that, I believed that being sensitive was bad and I shutdown my abilities in my teenage years.

"Over the next twenty-five years, I got married, worked, had kids and lived a pretty normal life.

"Early in 2012, I saw that I was able to have a positive impact on peoples' lives by using my psychic gift known as psychometry. Besides psychometry, while giving a 'reading,' I use clairvoyance, clairsentience, clairaudience and psychic sense of smell and taste. I have also had contact with relatives who have passed over, that wish to come through and show that life does indeed continue within the world of spirit.

"I am not in charge of the 'readings,' spirit is. I am only a channel to convey messages from guides and loved ones, from the other side.

"Coming out, about my abilities is the best thing that I ever did. No longer worried what others think of me, has opened a whole new world. It was as if spirit had been waiting for me to be ready. Now when strangers ask me what I do for a living I simply state, I am employed full time by spirit.

"In a 'reading' for *Bonnie, I saw that she was at a crossroads in her life. She was considering leaving her job but due to a financial situation found that hard to do. She did not know whether to stay in the job she currently had, or follow the path her heart was telling her to follow.

"Bonnie was highly intuitive, and saw herself standing on a stage or platform giving talks. I was told that she could do 'reading,' but was not sure that was where her heart was. It would be some income for her until later, but she would need to decide if she believed in herself enough to do 'readings'.

"I saw her writing several books that would make a difference to the world.

"Two relatives also came through, and they said she called them Nanna and Poppy. Nanna said Bonnie had been through some really hard yards in life, but she was over that now. Bonnie had learned her lessons, and now it was time to move on. The grandparents also said they were watching over her, and not to fear because they were never too far away. I also saw that her Poppy had worked for the railway.

"Two months later, Bonnie left the job and moved to a town that I saw as a stop-over, a place to learn some lessons before she moved on. Her ability to foresee things had scared her because some of the situations she saw were life events for friends, family that she had to go through. After explaining that we are only the messenger she has begun to work with her abilities.

"At the time of the 'reading', she was in the process of writing her first book and a sequel. My comments gave her the inspiration to continue on that path.

"Bonnie did call her grandparents Nanna and Poppy. She was happy to know that they watched over her as she had been very close to them, and yes, her grandfather did work for the railroad.

"*Tina was referred to me through a very close friend. This is a combination of what I saw and what has happened from two 'readings'.

"In the first 'reading,' I saw that Tina would move and be close to the water but that it would not be her final move.

"I saw several things in reference to her grandchildren and how grandchildren are very intuitive. I also saw disharmony and stress at certain work situations. Tina loved her work, but she had been under pressure to make the massive decision to move interstate to be closer to her family in Queensland.

"Tina did move to live seaside, quite literally on the beachfront for many months. Then she became seriously ill with a chest infection that stayed with her for months and time off work was a must.

"Then due to the sudden death of her son's mother- in-law, Tina's family wanted her to live closer to them. She told her son that she wanted to stay where she was and continue with work. However, shortly after that, she moved interstate to be with her family. The ocean is just one street away.

"After the first 'reading' I helped Tina with a long standing emotional relationship issue that had affected her life negatively for many years. She said that although she still remembers the events, she can no longer access the painful emotions that were associated with them.

"I have known *Candy for over ten years and have done several 'readings' for her over the years. She is also the one that encouraged me to become a professional psychic.

"I asked if she would share predictions that have happened over the years, and this is what she said.

"Denise has predicted everything from studying a new course to getting work in the field of that study, to later getting a promotion and branching out in new areas of the field that I work in.

"She predicted the birth of a new baby. Now one of my four daughters is just about to give birth to her first child making me a grandma for the first time. She predicted that her twin sister would excel in her chosen career working with horses, which now she does.

"She also spoke of a new relationship, the marriage that I was in, and that the marriage would consequently end.

"She spoke of the negative energy in which my former home held—fights that were had in the hallway of the home by previous tenants, and the portal energy that was in my eldest daughter's bedroom."

"*Nadine and I have also known each other for around ten years, and I believe her to be one of my spiritual teachers.

"Over the years, Nadine would ask me to hold her jewelry to read. She saw my potential, but she also saw the self-doubt and lack of confidence in my abilities. However, as a good teacher does, she persisted and continued to kick my butt. So over the years, Nadine and I have done many mini 'readings' and practice sessions together.

"Here are just some things Nadine shared.

"Denise described a lady and the dress the lady was wearing. It was my Nan that had come through. Denise made references to clouds. Nan's favorite saying was that she sat on cloud nine.

"In my 'readings', Denise showed me insecurities I had in my marriage, and that I was projecting these insecurities onto my husband. She taught me that those insecurities were really my own. That alone has helped in so many ways in how I now view and trust my marriage.

"I also learned that the terrible anxiety attacks I had, were not about me, it was the energies of everyone else that I was picking up on. With her help, I learned how to protect my energies to outside influences."

Chapter 12

Telepathic / Telepathy

Telepathy is the silent passing of information from one person to another. Silent is a key word because non-verbal communication can also be achieved through sight, audio, and touch. Body language can shout, and a locked jaw can speak volumes, but there are subtle differences to mind-to-mind telepathic communication.

If you asked married couple at a large gathering how they communicated without an eye roll or 'rescue me' expression to convey a thought, many couples would say there is a gut feeling, a flash of insight, or an inner voice, that without visual contact tells them that something is wrong.

If you asked a person forced to listen to a self-centered bore, what they were thinking while the person droned on about their latest accomplishment, vacation, or newest expensive gadget, many would admit to silently screaming, 'rescue me, save me, or get me out of here, now,' or similar thoughts.

The trapped person's thoughts are packed with energy and can be intercepted by anyone in the room, and very well may be. It is also possible that although several people 'hear' the plea, the only person willing to intervene is someone with an emotional stake in the distressed person's situation.

At school, a child feels ill. They think of a parent, older sibling or grandparent. The thought may be a direct plea, or a wishful thought, the process itself is a tool that allows thought energy (telepathic communication) to flow. Besides a gut feeling, the child's thoughts may echo through the receiver's thoughts. The receiver may smell a scent associated with the child, like strawberry shampoo or lip balm. Sadly, all too often the telepathic communication is ignored or dismissed as nonsense. Later in the day, when the child demands to know why everyone ignored his pleas to come to the school, the parent or guardian will still dismiss the idea that they heard the child's plea.

A daughter needs to talk to her mother, but they are not near a phone. Mentally, the daughter sends out the message, 'call me.' An hour later the phone rings, and the mother says she had a feeling to call.

A husband is at the grocery store when the wife realizes they need molasses to make cookies. The wife calls him, but the cellphone goes to voicemail and a message says the mailbox is full. When the man arrives home, there is a jar of molasses in the bag. He claims she told him to purchase the molasses.

Four men in a car pool seldom talked during the commute. One morning a passenger mentions something that the driver was also thinking about at that moment.

Incidences similar to these happen daily. Instead of recognizing the intuitive ability as telepathic communication, people laugh and call it a coincidence, dumb luck or a lucky guess.

During experiments for telepathic communication, people with telepathic abilities agreed to be locked in rooms thousands of miles apart. Isolated from sound and other humans, they drew pictures or wrote comments about what the other person was thinking or visualizing. Articles written about these telepathic experiments and other telepathic experiments, report that there were times the accuracy rates were high. Yet, scientists labeled a good portion of the correct answers as coincidental.

The idea of using telepathic communication for James Bond style espionage works well in a movie. In real life, the world knowing a person's every thought, transgression and desires would make life a living hell.

Fear of people reading your mind aside, everyone has the capacity to communicate telepathically. For most people the ability will be stronger between people with an emotional connection.

Using telepathic communication is as simple as a thought and a projection of desire—call me; a question—where are you; or a thought—buy butter. The receiver needs to accept that the communication is genuine, listen, and if necessary react.

Elena Skyhawk's life story is in chapter nine. This is a story she shared about her use of telepathic communication and healing energy with animals.

"One day, a young lady called me about her dog, *Daisy. She had been diagnosed with an inoperable brain tumor behind the left eye. The girl, a college student at the time, believed that energy healing could help Daisy.

"The young woman's mother was skeptical, but she flew to Arizona to attend the meeting.

"When I arrived at the house, I was introduced to Daisy, a beautiful three year old Golden Retriever.

"As with humans, animals need to understand what is happening, and give permission for me to work with them. Speaking aloud, so the dog's owners understood what was happening, I explained to Daisy what I would to do with her. However, first we had to address some other issues.

"Because of the tumor, Daisy had developed some bad habits, like not waking anyone up when she needed to go outside. I explained that that was not an option. Then, after explaining the procedure, we followed through with her actually moving from her dog bed to the bedroom where she would gently wake someone up.

"Daisy was eager to please, and we agreed to a three day regime of Shaman's Touch Healing, and Reiki.

"For two days, I used healing touch and moved healing energy through Daisy. After about an hour and a half, she would let me know she'd had enough, and would stand and walk away.

"On the third day, I moved healing energy through Daisy's body until she was drowsy. Simply stated psychic surgery is using energy to visualize the removal of the tumor. Daisy handled the energy very well, and again once, when she was ready she stood and left the room.

"Weeks later, Daisy had an appointment at the veterinary school where the tumor had been diagnosed. X-rays showed the tumor was shrunk to the size of a pea. The surgery to remove the tumor was not complicated and Daisy is happy, healthy and living a full life."

Colette St. Clair is a fascinating woman, with a wealth of information and passion for what she believes. Before using her intuitive gifts professionally, she held several interesting positions, including CEO for an industrial and agricultural machinery company. At one time, she worked in London for Merrill Lynch, as a financial consultant. She was certified with the NY Stock Exchange, and the Chicago Board of Trade. She graduated from the American University for Complimentary Medicine and has studied energy psychology, Reiki and finance.

Currently living in California, Colette's interests are diverse. It only takes a few minutes in her company to know that she takes her intuitive abilities seriously and hopes one day to work with doctors to help people with difficulty in communication.

In her words, this is her story.

"I grew up in Beirut, Lebanon. As a child I knew I was different, but there was not a good feeling about the differences.

"As a child, I not only had a connection with animals, but with young children, particularly those who were learning impaired or medically handicapped. Because I was empathic and clairsentient, in my late teens I started a different type of relationship with elderly people.

"Initially, I wanted to be a doctor. I started medical school, but was expelled because I refused to kill animals for the purpose of dissecting them. To me, if medicine was not advanced enough that we could bypass killing animals to learn, I was not going to do that.

"Knowing I had abilities started in1989. Prior to that, I knew I was different, but it wasn't necessarily feeling good about the differences.

"What I was going through was paratension; which is having knowingness, or having insight or intuition truly in the body. This happens through the body, because the body is one of the telepathic tools.

"I also experienced clairsentience as a child. I understood when I was listening to lies or false truths in general, but I did not understand that it was a psychic process that I was going through.

"The other thing I did as a child was communicate with our dogs, it was so second nature that I did not think twice about it. Of course, no member of my family believed that the information actually came from the dogs. They thought it was my projections, or I was saying things because it was what I wanted for them.

"The first time that I had a clear understanding and evidence that I was really practicing telepathy was in September 1989. I was living in London, and awoke from what I thought was a nightmare that my dog had died. In fact, when I opened my eyes my dog came to me and told me that she had died. She was on another continent with my family. She assured me that she was okay. She was the one who pointed out that I had something special to offer because I really had communicated with her. Several hours later, I called my parents, and they confirmed that my dog had died. She was only five and healthy, so this was not expected. Caught up in the grief of her death, I did not think too long and hard about what she said.

"The true practice began in 1994 with animals. This time with farm animals, but some house pets as well. Also, I started hearing the voices of people who had died, but had not fully crossed over. It evolved from there.

"When I arrived in the United States in 2000, I began with animal communication and very soon that unfolded into communication with living-beings.

"In the spring of 2003, I was in a café, with a friend and her toddler. Very young, she was just learning to walk, and she started talking to me. She complained about stuff that upset her, especially her mom reprimanding her for touching stuff that would potentially hurt her.

"Then I'm in a bank, and a child is sobbing, and I hear her say that she is in pain because she needs to poop, but she is constipated.

"Then I'm at a farm trying to work the animals, but a three and a half year old boy is sobbing. I tell the mother I cannot work until the boy is settled because he is upsetting the animals. Telepathically the boy explains to me that he understands why the father is not home enough. Mind you this was my first visit to the farm, and I knew nothing about the family situation. The mother was stunned that he understood so much.

"People are stunned that babies who cannot even say mama can communicate and understand what is going on around them. But let's face it; the mind is not the brain. It is dependent on the brain for proper functioning while we are alive, but even though I talk to the dead I am talking to the part of them that is a mental energy—their mind.

"To me it is no surprise that anything with a mind can talk, can communicate, but to most people that is crazy. Right now, I am in the process of trying to bring to doctors of natural medicine and holistic hypo therapist, the fact that telepathic communication is possible with people who have illnesses that prevent them from talking or being able to express their feelings. I am literally trying to get them to open their minds and use what I have to offer to investigate the health and wellbeing of these people. There is a lot of potential to bring to popular awareness that every human being has more than one cognitive mind, and have the capacity for the types of exercise that today people think only is possible from the realm of being a psychic.

"Still working with very young children I began to get more and more into working with people who cannot express themselves. Babies, autism, down-syndrome, dementia, stroke victims; I work with all of them. Also, I still do telepathic communication with dead people as well as dead animals.

"*Jane wanted me to talk to her deceased cat, but I felt the energy of a male spirit—the cat was female. What I was feeling was the energy of a spirit baby. Jane was not surprised as her therapist had said she felt Jane had a spirit baby attachment. The spirit was very impatient to be born, even though Jane was not married and had no immediate plans to marry or the desire to start a family.

"The spirit had been causing her discomfort in the sense that something was off, and she had felt like someone was continually watching her. The spirit had one goal—to be born, to reincarnate.

"He claimed he was a genius who had something important to offer the universe. He said he would not be an easy child, but he promised to reward her for facilitating his next life, but he only cared for himself.

"Jane told him she refused to give him birth. We worked on love life and personal life with family and her home. She lived in San Francisco where the fires were, so we needed to move ghosts. She was trying to sell her house, and she had an employee who was detrimental to the company. Using telepathic communication Jane talked to the employee. The employee shared her anger and resentment and why she was not working. The troubled woman made a full turn around and now there are no problems at work.

"Jane has transformed her life to being more open and accepting of herself and the people in her life, allowing awareness to guide her.

"We are nothing but spiritual plumbers—we clean out the pipes to help people's energy flow freely."

If I'm Crazy, I Am In Good Company

Chapter 13

Vision / Visual

Visions are intuitive visual scenes that offer a glimpse into past, present and future events. The difference between a vision and a daydream is that a person cannot control or change the scene, and a vision cannot be manifested at a whim.

If a person closes their eyes, and thinks of a fall day where the air snaps with cool energy they may see majestic oak trees covered in fall foliage, or a harvest moon shining on a scarecrow standing watch over bright orange pumpkins. They may also see an event from their past that represents fall. Whatever the vision, the process of taking conscious thought and tapping into the unconscious memory bank to create the visualization is effortless and instantaneous.

Another type of visualization is a flash card image produced by thoughts. The image is gone in a second, but the vision can coincide, or perhaps the vision prompts, a 3-D effect of sight, taste, smell and sound.

If you doubt that, think of a hot bubbling pizza and pay attention to whether or not your higher conscious added smell and taste to the vision. If you think of the INDY-500 races do you have an instant flash of the cars, track, engines roaring and crowds cheering?

Standing in a slow moving line at a coffee shop, seven women and six men answered these two questions; what is your favorite pizza, and have you ever been to or watched a stock car race on television. Then I asked if they visualized a pizza or race car when asked the questions. Everyone hesitated, before acknowledging that there was a quick vision, a vision that was not consciously acknowledged or noticed until asked.

A surprising result was that coinciding with the image of the race cars, audio perception was unanimous. All twelve people heard the whine of fine-tuned engines.

When asked to name their favorite pizza one person saw the pizza and smelled hot pepperoni, and one person smelled burnt cheese. Everyone said their mouths watered as the pizza's image flashed. So, even when the sense of smell was not evident, the vision of a pizza produced the subconscious reaction to produce saliva in preparation to eat.

The unique combination of car fumes, burning rubber, and concession stand food was limited to the four people who had attended drag races. A NASCAR enthusiast said he saw a flash vision of a checkered flag, and for a second felt the anticipation of a race starting.

The visions created through word association were automatic and until pressed to think about the matter, ignored. The same is true with intuitive visions. Unless they are Technicolor impressive, they can be ignored, or dismissed as a daydream or wishful thought.

A man who attended a hypnosis workshop shared that when he thought of his former wife, he imagined her has an old hag. He thought the vision was a daydream byproduct of an emotionally draining marriage and equally dramatic divorce. Several years passed without contact with the former wife, and then they both attended the funeral of a mutual friend. He said that without the visions, he would not have recognized her. Bitterness and illness had taken their toll, and shaped her into the image he had been seeing in the vision.

After that encounter, he paid closer attention to other visions. The visions lasted mere seconds, and happened only when he thought about a person he knew, or an event he would attend. By writing down what he saw, which was usually the image of one person, or a photo image of a room or outdoor scene, he realized that the visions offered him a glimpse into the future. The information was never about earth shattering events, or of interest to anyone else, but the visions forced an examination and adjustment to his beliefs.

For the person who receives insightful visions, pausing to examine and consider what the soul (subconscious) offers is a crucial step to acceptance and personal growth. Visions can be realistic detail orientated short clips of information. They can also be a snapshot, in black-and-white or color.

When a vision appears during a 'reading', or when talking to someone, I concentrate on the people in the vision first. Their clothing, hair styles, and furnishings help identify a timeframe. If the scene is outside, trees, sky and foliage can give clues to the time of the year and a possible location.

During hypnosis, self hypnosis and in dreams, people tend to see every nuance in a scene, or only the important details register. Either way, they receive the information needed.

In a vision, the details or omission of normal details in a setting are important clues to understanding the vision. The temptation to add something because it 'should' be there is normal, but undermines the information being presented.

For example, while talking to a friend, a vision of a bedroom materialized. There were dressers, nightstands, and a chaise lounge, but no bed. It would have been easy to assume the bed was out of sight, but to have said so would have altered what I saw and her perspective. The room did not connect with any of her memories until I mentioned there was a large statue of a nude male in a corner. The statue belonged to her sister. A call confirmed the bed had been removed because she wanted the space to do yoga. She slept on the chaise lounge.

As with any intuitive power, visions need to be interpreted by the intended receiver. If, while talking to a client, I see five men doing a line dance on my lawn, the client needs to decide what it means. Their questions or musings may generate another vision, but all I can do is enjoy the show and relate the details without embellishing the facts.

Visions - Meditation

If meditation conjures up thoughts of bodies twisted into a pretzel, closed eyes and humming off key, it is time to change the image because the real purpose of meditation is self awareness.

This is what Collette St. Clair, her story is in chapter thirteen, says about meditation. "…most people do not understand that the purpose of meditation is to de-clutter the mind. When you start meditation the computer of the mind starts to generate anything and everything that needs to be de-cluttered. People try to push it away, or they try to repress the thoughts, but they shouldn't because it defeats the purpose of meditation. They are supposed to acknowledge whatever thought is coming through and let it go.

"For example, when I start meditation I start getting thoughts of adding stuff to my grocery list or things I forgot to do, or I need to write this. Okay, this is my mind working, it is like a computer—defragmentation and looking for cookies and viruses and Trojans and getting rid of them. Allowing self to be rid of these thoughts, in order to clear the way to one's higher consciousness, people will find more truth about who they really are as well as the psychic and intuitive skills they have."

With the mind free of distractions, it is possible for answers to appear as visions. Maybe the vision is a simple snapshot of visiting a friend that will later nudge you to call the person and make a date to meet for lunch. During that lunch date, the person says something that opens a door to answers of a personal or business nature.

Answers are seldom straightforward, but with follow through on what the subconscious offers, answers are available. The trick is accepting that the answer is not always what we want to hear.

Types of Visions

Past

Past could mean yesterday, last week, last year, or a hundred years ago.

If reincarnation is not part of your beliefs, then a vision of a long ago event can be interpreted like a parable, a story with hidden meanings that will offer comfort and answers.

If reincarnation is part of your beliefs, it is possible the vision is a glimpse into a past life that connects to a current situation.

Seeing segments of the past can also clarify a fading memory, show personal growth, and illustrate a connection between a former and present situation.

Present

Visions that encompass an immediate situation or something that will happen within shortly are insight visions.

I have heard several people say they had visions of an auto accident minutes before the accident happened.

A neighbor was at work when he saw his wife lying on the couch cradling her belly. A call home confirmed she was in the first stage of labor.

Millie Gemondo had a vision of her husband having dinner with a female co-worker. Before the vision, he called to say he was having a drink at a local bar with the guys. When she confronted him he denied the accusation, but when doing the laundry she found a receipt for the restaurant in his pants pocket.

When an elderly neighbor died on Christmas morning I had a vision of her lying in bed, her husband sat beside her, crying. Walking next door, I arrived at the same time as the family minister.

Leaving work, a friend's sister told a co-worker that she had a vision of a man she had only dated twice proposing marriage. Later that evening, when the proposal became reality, she was prepared to say no without embarrassing either of them.

A present vision can also show insights into a person's character and help answer questions when dealing with people and unfamiliar situations.

Future

Having a crystal ball that accurately predicts the future is impossible, but many visions offer a glimpse into future events that happen weeks, months and years after the vision is documented.

Whether a 'reader' is telling a person about a vision or the person is receiving the vision, the information offers the opportunity to head down the same path or take a different direction. The ability to choose to continue forward, head due east, or turn south, is the main reason predictions about future events are seldom totally accurate.

Many visions, like those of Nostradamus, are shrouded inside stories that sound like they are scenes from a sci-fi novel. To accurately decipher the prediction, before the fact, is probably impossible.

Still, some visions are a warning to help people prepare for things they cannot change.

A year before World War I started, Millie Gemondo's mother started seeing a man standing in their front yard. Because he was wearing a uniform, she found the vision disturbing. When she told her parents she thought there was going to be a war, they told her to stop talking nonsense.

A vision of attending college may be confused with wishful thoughts or a daydream until the vision is played out in real time. One could argue that desire created action that produced the vision. However, if the vision had never shown the outcome of desire, the person may not have worked towards the goal.

In a reversal of that, a vision of a teenage pregnancy, a skiing accident or a blowout argument with a friend, may be avoided by making different choices. Notice I said maybe. Fate plays a part in everyone's life and even if different choices are made the outcome could be the same.

Like clairvoyants and mediums, an image of a snowman may be a visual symbol for cold, childhood fun or eating a snow cone. Word association, like the game kids play, and psychiatrist use to understand how we think, is a direct intuitive insight that links the subconscious and conscious thoughts.

For example, on a dreary overcast day, the vision of a plane streaking across a cloudless blue sky comes from the subconscious. Thoughts like, trip and vacation are conscious thoughts. A flight attendant may connect the plane to work. A pilot may feel the rush of anticipation that occurs in the first exhilarating second the plane lifts off the ground. A person wanting to escape a dreary winter may associate the plane with a trip to warmer weather.

If the message in the vision is connected to the thought, like a vision of a sandwich reminding a person that they are hungry, that is the end of the vision. However, there could be more to the message. The word association for the flight attendant is work. That word triggers a vision of a computer screen, and that reminds her that she forgot to log into the company website and print out her schedule.

Not all visions are easily answered or uncomplicated, so to expect instant answers with every vision is unrealistic. A typical scenario would be similar to this.

For me, a plane brings up many images. My father was a navigator in the Air Force. I have relatives who fly privately and in the military. When learning to fly, my first solo flight is a fond memory. Business trips and vacations are also associated with flying. So, answers could involve a business trip, a relative, vacation, my father or a father figure. Navigation could relate to driving to a new place, and solo flight could represent the need for time alone. If there was no obvious answer I would sit quietly, imagine the plane, and wait for the next thought or vision. If that produced no answers, I would write down the vision and the date, and wait.

The reason for writing everything down is straightforward; like most dreams, the memory of visions and intuitive insights fade. Within hours or days the information will be totally forgotten, or what little is remembered is distorted. At a later date, when reading the written account, the vision may reappear or the 'reading' generates another vision and more insight. Connecting the vision to something that has happened or is currently happening is also possible.

Intuitive visions are instant and seldom last more than a few seconds. The process is so natural that the visions and the process of what activated the memory is ignored and forgotten.

Similar to word association the vision can be symbolic. An apple tree, or pair of red glittery heels, will have significant meanings, and offer clues to an answer. Perhaps an apple represents health, or a wicked step-mother, like in the story Sleeping Beauty. For me, a shiny red apple represents breakfast. Red glittery heels could remind a person of the Wizard of Oz, fear, witches or home. For me, they represent the power within us.

Cars are often used as a symbolic message because the age, model, condition, and color can translate a lot of information quickly. Using the age and model of the car, the symbol could remind a person of Uncle Henry the family clown, which could lead to a different memory that holds the answers in the vision.

I met *Chris, an intuitive visionary, in Phoenix, Arizona. Managing a bar at the airport, he met people from all over the world. After he asked if a trip to Florida was for family or Disney World (it was both) I ask him how long he had been using his psychic abilities. With a three hour layover before my next flight, we had plenty of time to talk.

Chris was in his late twenties when he asked a couple if they enjoyed their cruise. The couple laughed and said it was a lucky guess, but it had not been a guess. While taking their drink orders, he had a vision of a tall white ship. When he delivered the drinks, he got a flash snapshot of a choppy ocean.

Shortly after that experience, he started to keep a diary of the quick snapshot style visions that showed an item or a place. Next to that he noted the accuracy of what he sensed the symbol or picture meant. At first his accuracy was in the low sixty percentile. By using the diary to see consistencies in what was shown and what they meant, his accuracy rate increased to the low nineties.

Vision can also appear as a fast paced scene, like a thirty second commercial that gives a detailed account of an event that can be from the past, the present or future. Audio details may or may not accompany the vision.

For me, snapshot visions are rare and usually are confirmed by the receiver as a picture of someone in their family. Recently a picture of a couple at their wedding was connected to the person's brother. The brother and his fiancé had decided to marry on their parents' thirtieth wedding anniversary. The man I was talking to had been asked, just that morning, to be in the wedding party.

Mini videos last a few seconds and are usually accompanied by an audio answer to a question. Usually the vision offers details that the 'voice within' does not include, but sometime the vision and audio are not related.

One day while giving a 'reading', I kept seeing a garden filled with flowers, but the questions I was being asked and the answers received were of a different nature. Finally, I mentioned the flowers and the woman said she was sitting on a deck watching a neighbor weed flowerbeds. With thoughts being energy, the vision showed me that her thoughts were not fully engaged in our conversation.

For the few seconds that a vision appears, the receiver's eyes will be unfocused and the surroundings become hazy. Once a vision is received it is like an imprint that can be recalled for a short time before fading from the memory.

Pictures, whether they are black-and-white or colored are clear, and the details never change. I mention that because all too often people think that if they ask a question a hundred different ways, visions can be altered to fit their wants.

It may be different for others, but for me, video style visions are not always crystal clear around the outer edges. That focuses my attention on the main action, and is probably why it is shown that way.

Even though the duration usually lasts only seconds, a mini scene can span a lot of time. Again, this is my experience and may be different for other people, but when sharing a vision, the scene reappears and sometimes more detail is shown.

Besides skepticism, a reason to hesitate before sharing what is shown is the person may not react favorably.

A good friend rented a room from a friend who also happened to be her employer. Several months into the arrangement, Stan proposed marriage. Linda turned him down, but he was persistent. One evening she asked if I saw them getting married. I said yes and explained what I was being shown. Linda trusted the vision, and it scared her to death. The next day she packed her bags and moved out.

Linda admitted Stan's persistence was wearing down her resistance, and she did not want that reality. We have joked that the vision was a wake-up call to get her to react as she did, and that may be the truth. Her decision to move out was a choice based on the vision because she did not want that reality. So, it is possible that the vision was the nudge needed to do what was best for her.

Visions can also be a message for someone the receiver knows. These are probably the most difficult visions to understand because unless the receiver knows the intended recipient well, approaching them with a story about a vision could be difficult.

A woman in Utah was given my name by a mutual friend. After talking to her for a few minutes, I saw a very clear vision of a couple in their mid to late twenties. The snapshot was black-and-white, but the uniform the man wore reminded me of a mailman or milkman. The woman's dress and hairstyle put the time frame in the 1940's to early 1950's. The woman's grandfather had been a mailman and from my description, she felt I was seeing her grandparents.

A few minutes later, I mentioned how much her son enjoyed riding the horses the woman trained. There was a pause before she said she had no son. Then she said her youngest daughter had been telling her stories about a boy who never left her bedroom. The girl said the boy slept on her head and she wanted him to stop.

As we talked, the scene of the nine or ten year old boy riding a horse and laughing kept returning. My 'voice within' offered no explanation. With no possible answer, she said she would talk to the owner of the property she rented.

A few days later, she called to say the property owner, a man in his late sixties, had built the house and raised his family on the property. He had also lost a son who loved horses. At the time of his death, the son was the age of the boy I saw in the vision. There could be another explanation for the boy the woman's daughter saw as a spirit and the one in the vision enjoying a horse ride, but believing in coincidence is for the foolish who do not want to believe or trust in intuitive powers.

Chapter 14

One Last Word

When asked if intuitive abilities are possible there are no fence sitters; people believe or they don't. People trust their intuitive instincts, or believe they could never process the ability.

Holding wind in my hand or locating the skunk that perfumed the air, are not necessary to know they exist. At the same time, my skeptic nature does not include the ability to deny what is obvious.

Trusting the intuitive abilities that are within us takes faith and the ability to see beyond the obvious. Questioning what is heard or seen is a healthy reaction, but denying the truth or refusing to consider the improbable as probable, shuts doors to possibilities and narrows the ability to find answers that very well may enrich one's life.

Along with faith in yourself, accept that not everyone will believe your truths. Not everyone will want to hear about intuitive awareness, and not everyone will be polite when they state their thoughts. When hurtful and negative comments are made to your face, and behind your back, remember that everyone is entitled to their beliefs.

A person can bet money on predictions not always being stellar perfect. When that happens do not let that moment define who you are and don't question the natural, God given powers within you. If you stuck to the facts, without embellishing for the sake of making a look at me statement, there is no reason to second guess intuitive powers or apologize. The truth will present itself in time or through choices the person makes, the outcome will change.

This book has offered a glimpse into my life, and the lives of other highly intuitive, professionals who also use their skills and knowledge to help others. What we experience will parallel some of your experiences, but like a fingerprint, no two people have the same exact abilities, capabilities or interests.

Do not judge yourself against someone else. How you embrace and use your intuitive abilities is perfect, for you.

Life is a large classroom, where hopefully, with only a little prodding we learn something useful that can be shared and eventually passed down to the next generation. If this book made you think, consider possibilities, or accept concepts and ideas you never thought possible, become the teacher and share the information. Like the decision to read this book, age, financial status, where a person lives and education do not matter. When the time is right for a person to learn, explore possibilities and learn lessons, opportunities are presented.

Trust in yourself, and enjoy the journey,
Rhonda

In Alphabetical Order - Directory of Contributors

Simone Browne
Australia
Website: www.simonebrownepsychic.com/
Facebook:
www.facebook.com/SimoneBrownePsychicMedium

Marcey Hamm
Texas
Founder of: Waha Topa Inc.
Website: musicbymarcey.com

Nand Harjani
California / Hong Kong
Founder of: Creative Life Science
Website: creativelifesciences.com

Millie Gemondo
West Virginia
To contact Millie please go to irplummer.com and email me for the information

Denise Lambie
Australia
Website: www.denisethedreamcatcher.com

Tracy Lee Nash, E.H.P.
California
Founder of: Within The Light
Website: www.withinthelight.com

I. R. (Rhonda) Plummer

Idaho
Founder of: Path to Inner Awareness
Website: www.irplummer.com

Elena Skyhawk

Arizona
Website: www.spiritual-shaman.com

Colette St. Clair

California
Website: www.mysticlanguages.com
Facebook:
www.facebook.com/ColetteStClairPsychicTelapathicExpert

David Tillman

California
Website: www.psychicdave.com

Gavin van Vuuren

Australia
Website: www.spirit-consciousness.com
Facebook: www.facebook.com/iamspiritconsciousness

References:

Psychic - Merriam-Webster Dictionary
www.merriam-webster.com/dictionary/psychic

Natural Law – New World Encyclopedia
www.newworldencyclopedia.org/entry/natural_law

Stages of Sleep
www.psychology.about.com
www.sleepdex.org/stages
www.healthcommunities.com/sleep-stages
www.world-of-lucid-dreaming.com
www.dreamviews.com/content/sleep-stages

Quotes - Intuition
www.brainyquote.com/quotes/intuition
www.quotegarden.com/intuition
www.searchquotes.com/quotes/about/Intuition

Quotes - Dreams
www.quotationspage.com/subjects/dreams

Sigmund Freud
www.library.thinkquest.org
www.psychology.about.com/freud
www.dreaminterpretation-dictionary.com

Abe Lincoln Dream
www.rogerjnorton.com/Lincoln

Reticular Activating System (RAS)
www.innovateus.net/health/what-function-reticular-
activating-system
www.psychologydictionary.org/

Joseph Rodes Buchanan – psychometry
www.fst.org/buchanan.htm

www.ingramcontent.com/pod-product-compliance
Lightning Source LLC
Chambersburg PA
CBHW030916090426
42737CB00007B/214